Abandonment Theology

The Clergy and the Decline
of American Christianity

John W. Chalfant
President
America - A Call to Greatness, Inc.

DEDICATION

There is a remnant of great clergymen and millions of grassroots American citizens who have refused to succumb to the onslaught of secularism and its myriad of freedom-destroying New Age cults. Fearless and in good faith, these gallant men and women fight on today, carrying the banner of Christ - the Hope of America, of our children and of the world - onto all of the battlefronts.

This book is dedicated to those gallant clergymen and all Americans who as "salt" and "light" forge ahead in defense of our nation's God-given freedoms.

ACKNOWLEDGMENTS

This book, the first of a series, is the result of the work of hundreds of men and women in a multiplicity of support efforts including Internet marketing and the production of network video specials.

It would be impossible to show proper appreciation for all of them in this short book, but the story is told and a number of them are named in "Acknowledgments," Appendix D.

Special thanks to my editor, Dr. Lila Buchanan, for guiding the task through to completion.

Contents

INTRODUCTION

CHAPTER ONE
WHERE WE'VE BEEN:
STRONG SPIRITUAL ROOTS

CHAPTER TWO
THE DECLINE BEGINS:
A FORMULA FOR DESCENT

CHAPTER THREE
MILITARY VULNERABILITY

CHAPTER FOUR
DISARMING OUR MILITARY
FROM WITHIN

CHAPTER FIVE
THE NATURE OF THE STRUGGLE

CHAPTER SIX
ALL NATIONS THAT FORGET GOD

CHAPTER SEVEN
DISCOVERING BIBLICAL SOLUTIONS

CHAPTER EIGHT
WHAT WILL IT TAKE TO SAVE OUR COUNTRY?

APPENDIX A - PART ONE
THE PERSON OF CHRIST

APPENDIX A - PART TWO

APPENDIX B

APPENDIX C

APPENDIX D

FIGURES

INTRODUCTION

America Today

America is in serious trouble. In fact, while our government repeatedly assures us that we are at peace, our national survival is in peril. Most people sense it. Some are keenly aware of it. But few understand what the battles are all about, much less how to identify our enemies and their strategies of attack against our vital institutions of freedom. Few understand what it's leading to and the consequences to our country and posterity if our enemies aren't stopped. Furthermore, still fewer know how to stop them. That's what this book is all about.

The subtitle on the cover promises it to be:

An Action Guide To Save America.

You will find in this book the answers to these and other questions:

- "Abandonment" theology? What has been abandoned?

- What has been the source of America's great strength since her birth?

- Why does America, which has long been heralded as a great nation, need to be called to greatness? What *is* greatness? And why now?

1

- What does the contemporary clergy have to do with the decline of American Christianity and the increasing loss of our freedoms?

- For years we have been told by our government that America is "the most militarily powerful nation on earth." Is that still true? If not, why not?

- Is America actually under attack? If so, who are her enemies and what are their objectives? What are their strategies? Why are their attacks being waged on so many fronts? Why are we so vulnerable on these fronts?

- In the absence of a Spiritual renewal, what fate awaits us? How soon?

- What can we - you and I - do to save our country?

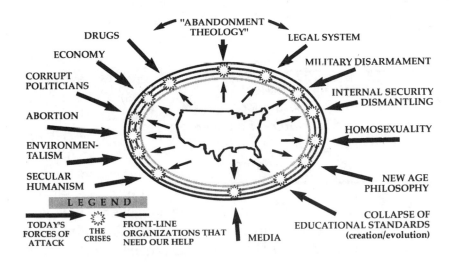

Figure 1.   The Consequences of Abandonment Theology

Figure 1 illustrates the consequences of Abandonment Theology. The large, attacking arrows symbolize the relentless attacks upon our vital institutions by those whose collective success will destroy America's sovereignty and force her into a one-world government.

The small, defending arrows symbolize the numerous organizations valiantly trying to sustain our freedoms and slow the decline and weakening of America's traditions and institutions which are founded upon Christian principles.

The concentric circles represent the battlefronts. They reveal a gradual collapse of our freedoms.

The all-encompassing lateral arrows extending from "Abandonment Theology" mean that in the Bible God speaks to every issue and offers all answers, but America is abandoning Him.

As this book demonstrates, America has turned her back on God. Figure 1 depicts the consequences and impending collapse of America's defenses which are accelerating toward a critical condition and, unless reversed, may result in the *sudden* loss of our remaining freedoms.

The Christian Worldview, with all of its components operating in tandem and harmony, has been our fortress of greatness, vision and invincible strength.

If Christians were obeying God, the arrows would be reversed. Those inside the circles would be large and bold and would represent America's Christians defending our God-given liberties as they repel and turn back the small, weaker, attacking arrows. God gave America's Christians that power and ability.

Giving Figure 1 movement in your imagination, what conclusion can you draw? The obvious answer is that America must aggressively take corrective measures on many battlefronts.

What can we do? We must obey God and engage in the fight as He commands us to do. Victory can be ours! That's God's promise to the faithful.

This book reveals the cataclysm brought about by Abandonment Theology and what can and must urgently be done if we are to save our country.

What Is Abandonment Theology?

Abandonment Theology is a term devised by the author to describe a faith which deceptively pawns itself off as Christianity by operating in the name of Christ but which produces fruits destructive to America's God-given freedoms. It comprises what is left today of the militant, power-filled, full-dimensional Christian faith of America's Founders after decades of erosion, watering down and trivializing of God's action mandates by America's Abandonment Clergy. It is a "feel good" theology that patronizes Jesus Christ and thereby gains legitimacy while at the same time produces disobedience to the commands of God and desertion of Christian duty.

Abandonment Theology is so deadly that we are losing our liberties, and evil is triumphing in nearly every aspect of life. A terrible spiritual blindness has come over millions of unsuspecting, victimized Christians who in turn have even allowed God, the Author of our liberties, to be in effect outlawed in our nation's public schools and institutions.

> *Abandonment Theology is so deadly that we are losing our liberties, and evil is triumphing in nearly every aspect of life.*

Through decades of erosion, the Abandonment Clergy have succeeded in extracting from the Christian faith the teeth of vigilance, of action, of obedience to God. If the clergy taught their flocks to *Fear God, and keep his commandments: for this is the whole duty of man* (Eccl. 12:13), America would not be plunging into the dark abyss as she is doing today. Why? Because, as Figure 1 shows, God speaks to every one of those named issues and sets the course for victory. If you were America's enemy, wouldn't you try to get rid of God, too, starting with the schools?

How have the Abandonment Clergy managed to triumph over such a nearly invincible heritage given to every American? This book deals with that subject in detail.

This book tells how it happened and reveals the central role of America's clergy in opening the floodgates to the archenemy of America's God-given freedoms. With the exception of an ever-faithful remnant, it was and is the clergy who have led the assault on the powerful, vigilant faith of the Founding Fathers who gave us our mighty, once-invincible American Constitutional Republic. Called the Abandonment Clergy, the theology they preach under the deceiving cloak of true Christianity can rightly be termed **Abandonment Theology.**

What does Figure 1, the total picture, represent in terms of the nature of the battles and of what's actually under attack? The answer is that the total war is essentially spiritual and ideological. "This world is a battlefield in the arena of ideas."[1] The battles are for the minds and hearts of the American people, especially her youth. The objective of our enemies is to render in shambles the Christian or Biblical Worldview which, with all of its components operating in tandem and harmony, has been our fortress of greatness, vision and invincible strength.

What does the Bible warn? *For when they shall say, Peace and safety; then sudden destruction cometh upon them...* (I Thess. 5:3). Many Bible scholars are prone to think "sudden" implies a nuclear first-strike. Not necessarily! It could mean the sudden collapse of America's pillars of liberty together with the will of her citizens, under a nuclear blackmail ultimatum. As you will see in reading this book, that scenario *is* possible. Today, God is calling America's Christians and all of her citizens to greatness as never before.

The Turning Point

In 1947 U. S. Supreme Court Justice Hugo Black lifted out of context a clause in President Thomas Jefferson's letter to the Danbury Baptist Association and used it in the case of *Everson v. Board of Education* to fabricate a two-way "wall of separation" between church and state.[2] Black thus laid the groundwork for abdication by America's clergy from leading their followers in their sacred duty to watch over the morals of their elected political representatives and to elect righteous men to office. God was shown the door, and "fallen human nature" took His place.

America was set for the ultimate test. Excepting a remnant, the Abandonment Clergy, fearing controversy, looked away in the Everson case and remained mute. They focused on teaching the social gospel and began their retreat to their non-controversial, profitable reservations.

> *Black thus laid the groundwork for abdication by America's clergy from leading their followers in their sacred duty to watch over the morals of their elected political representatives and to elect righteous men to office.*

The year was 1962 when America officially turned her back on God, as you will learn in Chapter Two. Soon thereafter, chaos broke out in almost every aspect of life. Morality ceased to be a tutor of behavior, violent crime soared, education plummeted to mediocrity, and the President of the United States introduced to the United Nations an upgraded plan for disarming our country and our people and surrendering America's sovereignty to the UN and its foreign military occupation forces.

In 1962 the extent of the triumph of the Abandonment Clergy in desensitizing America's Christians was put to the test in the landmark U.S. Supreme Court case *Engel v. Vitale.* This set the precedent for the 1963 case *Abington Township v. Schempp* which outlawed "unconstitutional" prayer and Bible reading in our nation's schools. This was followed by a series of similar cases until ultimately, in 1980 in *Stone v. Graham,* the court outlawed even the posting of the Ten Commandments in the public schools. After unsuccessful protest from the remnant, America's uncomprehending Christians let it happen.

Once God was shown the door, America went into chaos. Scholastic Aptitude Test scores plummeted. Violent crime rocketed upward. The abortion mills did an unprecedented business as they devised ever-more sadistic ways to kill children before and even during birth. Bill Clinton, elected President of the United States in 1992, aggressively advocated homosexuality,

> *God was shown the door, and "fallen human nature" took His place.*

which God calls "abomination." The Abandonment Clergy and their millions of undiscerning followers stood mute while America's sudden loss of greatness became obvious even to the world.

Incredibly, this was the ultimate hour for the Abandonment Clergy to see the light of truth. They faced blatant godlessness at every turn. They could have abandoned their own ways and made a comeback to the faith of the Founding Fathers. But what did they do?

They observed the horrible, deteriorating conditions in America, determined that she was headed into rubble just like ancient pagan Rome and that we must be living in the prophesied "last days" and "end times." Therefore, with the end and the "rapture of the church" so apparently near, why fight? "After all," these clergymen said, "We're in this world, not of it, so to heck with it," and "Compared to eternity we're here only for an instant." They told us that all that really counts is that we "lead as many people as possible to salvation and let our corrupted country continue on its death course."

Just what is the extent of the danger today, you ask? Do you realize that tens of millions of innocent men, women and children in cities throughout America could be incinerated by nuclear warheads or die horrible deaths from chemical or biological weapons delivered by Intercontinental Ballistic Missiles (ICBMs), and there is nothing we could do, even with advance notice, but watch the missiles come in? Why are our people unprotected? Because our government's legacy and continuing policy is that of "no defense" against attacking missiles.

Do we have the technology to develop interceptors capable of attacking and destroying the ICBMs from wherever they are launched in the world? Yes, we do, but policy says NO. Is it madness or something else? You will find the answer in this book.

America's millions of Christians who have been victimized by the Abandonment Clergy are actually well-meaning in their hearts. They love Christ, their children and their country, and they are among the finest people God ever created. If they understand their victimization, they can be brought back into the full-dimensional Christian faith. Then they will gladly *Put on the whole armour of God...* (Eph. 6:11) and get out on the battlefront where they know in their hearts they belong.

Nobody wants to lose freedoms or to usher his or her children and loved ones into the inferno. They just don't know what to do. Certainly Jesus, Who set the example for us in all of His conduct, was no pacifist: *For this purpose the Son of God was manifested that he might destroy the works of the devil* (I John 3:8). This book sets forth a number of the battle cries of Jesus that you rarely hear from the Abandonment Clergy.

Only by abdication of duty through disobedience to God do we lack the power to be victorious on all fronts of conflict, both spiritual and temporal. Christ gave us that power through the Holy Spirit. *Behold, I give unto you power to tread on serpents and scorpions, and over all the power of the enemy: . . .* (Luke 10:19).

It seems as if everybody senses that something is desperately wrong. Although many are resigned to accepting the year 2000 as roughly when Armageddon will take place and Christ will return (according to the Abandonment Clergy), those same Christians, given a Biblically justifiable alternative such as *Occupy till I come* (Luke 19:13), will gladly turn back to God,

> *The Abandonment Clergy have inverted God's Word to serve Satan's purpose.*

trust Him to intercede as He has promised and selflessly give the best that is in them to Him and, through Him, to America. This book has as its goal to turn the spotlight of God's truth on the areas where the Abandonment Clergy have disregarded the underlying fighting spirit of America's Christians and inverted God's Word to serve Satan's purpose.

Abandonment Theology, packed with the Word of God, presents the only authority that counts. The chapters include numerous quotations from God Himself Who tells us that it is He, not we, Who will determine when it is too late for America, that all events are in His control and that He is still willing to *heal our land* (II Chron. 7:14) *if* we will meet His conditions.

What can you and I do? Where can we turn for help? What actions can we take *today* to get started? Who are some of our most effective battlefront warriors? How can we help them and how can they help us? It's all in *Abandonment Theology.*

The Call and Way to Greatness

There is only one way out of the hole we have dug for ourselves, but it requires responding to the call – the Call to Greatness.

At the end of the Revolutionary War, George Washington, upon disbanding his army, called America's citizens to display true greatness. He said:

> They [the citizens of America] are from this period to be considered as the actors on a most conspicuous theatre, which seems to be peculiarly designated by Providence for the display of human greatness and felicity. Here they are not only surrounded with everything, which can contribute to the completion of private and domestic enjoyment, but Heaven has crowned all its other blessing, by giving a fairer opportunity for political happiness, than any other nation has ever been favored with...[3]

Washington called the American people to greatness as he acknowledged the Source of their (and our) blessings.

Exactly What Is "Greatness"?

The key to true greatness, that is, in this case, to saving America, is to *Draw nigh to God, and he will draw nigh to you* (James 4:8). To "draw nigh" is a total commitment which must be made by America's Christians to love the Lord and obey Him: *Jesus said unto him, Thou shalt love the Lord thy God with all thy heart, and with all thy soul, and with all thy mind.* (Mat. 22:37). Jesus declared: *This is the first and great commandment* (Mat. 22:38). There can be no higher priority.

Fear God, and keep his commandments: for this is the whole duty of man (Eccl. 12:13).

And in Response to Greatness

God, in turn, has promised to re-infuse us with the energizing power of the Holy Spirit, thus opening our eyes so that we may understand the urgency of the hour, the nature of the battles, what actions to take, how to be victorious and have the courage and power to do what must be done.

Sounding America's Call to Greatness and lighting the way to victory are the tasks of this book.

CHAPTER ONE

WHERE WE'VE BEEN:
STRONG SPIRITUAL ROOTS

Where the Spirit of the Lord is, there is liberty.
II Corinthians 3:17

Our Founding Fathers' Faith

Let's begin with the basic premise that our country's Founding Fathers were committed Christians and that they founded America and the freedoms of her citizens upon Biblical principles. They gave us:

> The world's greatest political success formula. In a little over a century, this formula allowed a small segment of the human family - less than six percent - to become the richest industrial nation on earth. It allowed them to originate more than half of the world's total production and enjoy the highest standard of living in the world. It also produced a very generous people. No nation in all the recorded annals of the past has shared so much of its wealth with every other nation as has the United States of America.[4]

Volumes have been written about America's countless blessings. Who else can claim freedom of worship and the freedom of the individual to rise as far as his or her talents allow in the pursuit of happiness? Prior to the miracle of the founding of the American republic, the

world's blood-drenched history was mostly characterized
by slavery, despotism and tyranny. The blessings of
liberty were inconceivable by both subject and ruler.

And yet, a nation of subjects unschooled in political
affairs created a government which was the servant of
the people. America's Christian citizens, beginning with
the Pilgrims in 1620, made God's Word the very center of
their personal and political lives. They taught their
children from their earliest years to read the Bible as the
infallible Word of God, to seek its knowledge, wisdom and transforming Spiritual power and to learn its great moral principles and God's laws of freedom.

The life, the light and the passion of Christ were part of their very makeup. Those children became the Fathers of America.

By the time of the Revolution in 1776, two generations of children had been steeped in the "Sacred Writ."
The life, the light and the passion of Christ were part of
their very makeup. Those children became the Fathers of
America.

The Fathers were of various denominations. They
long debated how to achieve certain political results. In
the end they, together with the citizens and the clergy,
were bound with solidarity in three basic beliefs: that
Jesus Christ is Lord and Savior; that He is the Author
and Grantor of liberty; and that the Bible is the ultimate
authority on civil government. Thus the Declaration of
Independence and the U.S. Constitution, which transformed civil government into the servant of the people
and the people into the master, became the most revolutionary political documents in all of history.

The Dual Nature of America's Self-Government

Why did the Declaration of Independence and the Constitution work? Why didn't this new nation, America, simply engage in a power struggle at the top, as did so many other nations such as France (in the wake of the French Revolution), and degenerate into despotism?

Typically, when oppressed people revolt and overthrow their oppressors, they form a "pure democracy," a type of self-government which functions on the rule of "50% plus 1." Often termed a "mobocracy," a pure democracy has no standard of justice or fairness, and 51% of the people voting as a mob can impose horrible injustices upon innocent victims. A pure democracy unbridled and uncontrolled is one of the worst and most unstable form of government. Karl Marx favored such democracies because they could readily be converted into socialism and then into communism. As he said in the *Communist Manifesto,*

> ...The first step in the revolution by the working class ... is to win the battle of democracy.[5]

Fisher Ames, who was responsible for writing the First Amendment to the United States Constitution, summed it up in these words:

> Liberty never yet lasted long in a democracy; nor has it ever ended in anything better than despotism.[6]

James Madison, writing one of the *Federalist* papers in 1787, argued for the Constitution by saying:

> ...Democracies have ever been found incompatible with personal security or the rights of prop-

erty;... and have in general been as short in their
lives as they have been violent in their deaths.[7]

There was not one man among the Founding Fathers
who wanted a democracy. Thus, when we are told by our
government that the American form of government is a
democracy, that statement is not true.

Aside from their observations of history, by what
authority did the Founding Fathers utterly reject democracy as being unworkable as a form of government? It is
vital that we understand *why* this was so, in order that
we fully appreciate the miraculous freedom-producing
self-government which the Fathers gave us in our American Constitutional Republic.

In the Bible Jeremiah describes the "fallen nature"
of man: *The heart is deceitful above all things, and
desperately wicked:*...(Jer. 17:9).

The Founding Fathers, being overwhelmingly Christians and advocates of a Christian Worldview, accepted
the Biblical account of the creation and the "fall," that
man can be described as possessing a "fallen nature," or
"sin nature," and that, as Jeremiah said, his heart is truly
desperately wicked. Founder John Adams expressed it in
these words:

> There is no reason to believe the one much more
> honest than the other. They are all of the same
> clay; their minds and bodies are alike...as to
> usurping others' rights, they are all...equally
> guilty when unlimited in power...The people,
> when they have been unchecked, have been as
> unjust, tyrannical, brutal, barbarous and cruel
> as any king or senate possessed of uncontrolled
> power. The majority has eternally, without one
> exception, usurped the rights of the minority.[8]

In forming a new government that would free men from political tyranny, the Founders had to contend with serious issues of power versus freedom. Was it actually possible to establish a government which guarantees freedom to the individual citizen and places responsibility upon him or her for overseeing that government, yet creates a structure that checks both the citizens' and their government's propensity for power and enslavement of their fellow man?

If you had lived during the time the Declaration of Independence and Constitution were being formed and knew the tyrannical history of nations and man's fallen nature, what would you have said when the Fathers declared the answer to political freedom to be *self-government?* On the surface it would have seemed ludicrous because it sounds like just another uncontrolled free-for-all barbaric democracy. But it was not.

Why? Because there was a

> *In forming a new government that would free men from political tyranny, the Founders had to contend with serious issues of power versus freedom.*

great bonding agent that existed between the several million citizens of the thirteen colonies, the clergy and their political representatives, who were almost entirely vigilant Christians. That bonding agent was the Bible, which they all considered to be the inspired, infallible Word of God, the absolute and final authority on all Spiritual, governmental (civil) and moral issues.

The political representatives of the citizens pledged their loyalty to the Bible. In fact, some states wrote that requirement for legislators into their constitutions. All delegates, including supposed "deists" Franklin and Jefferson, were outspoken in their Christian Worldviews. Most of them, though of various denominations, were Calvinists. Dr. John Calvin had bridged Christians and denominations together through his *Institutes of Christian Religion,* which brought the Scriptures into the realm of practical applications termed "The Four Great Dimensions of Life: Religion, Political Foundations, Economics, and Education."

The citizens, the clergy and their political representatives believed that the will of God, specifically of Christ, was that men should enjoy personal freedom and that spiritual and political bondage were of Satan. The task became to search the Scriptures for God's civil laws of government and to adapt them by framing a republic which would achieve permanent freedom for the individual, despite his underlying, inherited fallen nature.

The Declaration

Thus the Declaration of Independence was written, which set forth the dignity of every man and his God-given (not state-given) right to be free to enjoy "certain unalienable rights among which are life, liberty and the pursuit of happiness." (Happiness cannot be guaranteed, but it can be pursued in an atmosphere of political freedom.) This was, in reality, the essence of Jesus Christ's mission which He set forth in His mission statement (See Luke 4:18).

In effect, the Declaration of Independence, approved by the delegates on July 4, 1776, is an expression of *why* men have a right to be free, and it declares as its authority the Author of all freedoms and blessings, the Creator Himself.

When in the course of human events, it becomes necessary for one people to dissolve the political bands which have connected them with another, and to assume among the powers of the earth, the separate and equal station to which the Laws of Nature and of Nature's God entitles them...

We hold these truths to be self-evident, that all men are created equal; that they are endowed by their Creator with certain unalienable Rights; that among these are Life, Liberty, and the pursuit of Happiness; that to secure these rights, governments arc instituted among men, deriving their just powers from the consent of the governed; that whenever any form of government becomes destructive of these ends, it is the right of the people to alter or abolish it.[9]

"... that to secure these rights, governments are instituted among men, ..." is a derivative of Romans 13:1 through 4 in the Bible. This places government directly under the authority of God. At the time the Declaration was written, the phrase "the laws of Nature and of Nature's God" had only one reference, the God of the Old and New Testaments.

The Revolutionary War, that is, the War for Independence, was not just a rebellion against a governing authority, England, by people who simply wanted to govern themselves. More importantly, the war was a struggle to regain the God-given rights that King George was taking from the colonial people and to preempt their subjugation under what they termed in the Declaration an "absolute Tyranny over the states."

On July 3, 1776, the day following the approval by Congress of the Declaration of Independence, John Adams wrote to his wife, Abigail:

I am apt to believe that it will be celebrated by succeeding generations as the great anniversary Festival. It ought to be commemorated, as the day of deliverance, by solemn acts of devotion to God Almighty.[10]

As the Declaration was being signed by the members of the Continental Congress on August 2, 1776, Samuel Adams declared:

> We have this day restored the Sovereignty to Whom all men ought to be obedient. He reigns in heaven and from the rising to the setting of the sun, let His kingdom come.[11]

Most wars have their mottoes. We're all familiar with "Remember the Alamo!" The motto of the American Revolution was: "No king but King Jesus!"

Actually, the clearest perspective regarding what was happening - of the peoples' impending enslavement and the Biblical justification for the Revolution - is set forth by Patrick Henry in his fiery "Give me liberty, or give me death!" oration of March 28, 1775 before the Virginia Convention of Delegates. The notable fact about that speech, which helped to inspire the Declaration of Independence, is that it dealt in God's eternal absolutes of truth, liberty, and political thought, which apply to America today:

> The question before the House is one of awful moment to this country. For my own part, I consider it as nothing less than a question of freedom or slavery; ... It is only in this way that we can hope to arrive at truth, and fulfill the great responsibility which we hold to God and our country...

> They are sent over to bind and rivet upon us those chains which the British ministry have been so long forging...Shall we gather strength by irresolution and inaction? Shall we acquire the means of effectual resistance by lying supinely on our backs, and hugging the delusive phantom of hope, until our enemies shall have

bound us hand and foot?... There is no retreat but in submission and slavery! Our chains are forged! Their clanking may be heard on the plains of Boston!... It is in vain...to extenuate the matter. Gentlemen may cry peace, peace - but there is no peace. The war is actually begun. The next gale that sweeps from the north will bring to our ears the clash of resounding arms!...Why stand we here idle? ...What is it that gentlemen wish? What would they have? Is life so dear, or peace so sweet, as to be purchased at the price of chains and slavery? Forbid it, Almighty God! I know not what course others may take; but as for me, give me Liberty, or give me Death![12]

While today's manner of delivering this message may be different, the thrust of the warning is the same. The call is still being made today to the American people through this book and by many front-line organizations.

The Declaration echoed Patrick Henry's affirmation that man has a God-given right to be free. It further stipulated that "Government derives its just powers from the consent of the governed." Thus the Declaration laid the groundwork for the Constitution and for self-government by the people.

The Constitution

The Constitution of the United States, September 17, 1787, which followed the triumphant War for Independence, was based upon the Declaration of Independence. Its Preamble recites:

We the people of the United States, in order to...secure the blessings of liberty to ourselves and our posterity...

It became the legal instrument by which our God-given freedoms were set forth article by article and guaranteed. The Fathers first put all of the proposed articles of the Constitution to the Biblical test. Every article and every amendment in the Bill of Rights have their roots in the Bible. Had this not been the case, they would never have made it into the Constitution.

Some people ask why the Constitution does not mention God. That wasn't its purpose. The relationship between God and the people was mentioned four times in the Declaration. In effect, the Constitution does mention God in its Preamble

> *Under our Christian-based Constitution the citizens are charged with the sacred duty of vigilantly watching over their political representatives and of holding them accountable for their public moral conduct and their adherence to Biblical principles in all legislative matters.*

because everyone considered "the blessings of liberty" to have only one source - God, Himself. A number of the Fathers who signed the Constitution also had signed the Declaration. It was not necessary to re-identify the Author of liberty and the blessings which flow therefrom. The Declaration is the wellspring of the Constitution. They go hand-in-hand.

The Constitution is a document of law which implements the God-given rights of the citizens which were established in the Declaration and enumerated in the source book, the Bible. The Bible, the Declaration, and the Constitution comprise a cohesive trinity.

The Bible establishes government as the servant of the people, its purpose being to defend and protect them (See Rom. 13:1-4), not to enslave them. The Fathers knew that government, because of man's fallen nature, can become a terror to the people, so in the Constitution the government's powers had to be limited. They searched the Scriptures and in Isaiah 33:22 discovered the principle of "checks and balances" which they termed the "Separation of Powers":

> *For the Lord is our judge* (establishing the judiciary);
> *the Lord is our lawgiver* (establishing the legislature);
> *the Lord is our king* (establishing the executive).

In effect, the government was placed in competition with itself. If one branch attempted to acquire too much power, it could be overruled or balanced by another branch.

This was the first government in history that was founded upon the concept that man is a fallen creature with a propensity toward power and despotism but who, if controlled under a system of checks and balances, could enjoy God's purpose through his freedom.

Thomas Jefferson, recognizing man's irresistible quest for power and thus his underlying threat to freedom, said, "In questions of power, then, let no more be said of confidence in man, but bind him down from mischief by the chains of the Constitution."[13]

What, therefore, is America's *self-government?* The term sounds singular but actually has a dual meaning.

Our Bible-based Constitution has been recognized as the finest document for self-rule that has ever been put together. Its role is to limit the power of government and let the people be free to rule themselves.

Rather than a democracy, America's government is a republic in which the people elect those who will represent them in performing the functions of government. Under our Christian-based Constitution, the citizens, in exchange for their God-given freedoms, are charged with the sacred duty of vigilantly watching over their political representatives and of holding them accountable for their public moral conduct and their adherence to Biblical principles in all legislative matters. If a political representative steps out of bounds, he or she may be recalled by the people and discharged or voted out of office.

Therefore, the citizens are self-governing inasmuch as they hold the ultimate power over the political government. But how can a citizen unschooled in legislative matters govern a legislator especially in matters of economics, war and other issues that require specialized knowledge?

In colonial days the average citizen had been reared in the Scriptures. The literacy rate was nearly 100%. His handbook of freedom, which is also the greatest political handbook ever written, was the Bible, and most citizens owned one. The civil and moral laws of freedom are clearly and simply set forth in the Scriptures so that the average person can understand them.

Thus it was well within the ability of the colonial citizen to monitor his political representatives and hold them accountable to God's laws of freedom. A citizen did not have to be skilled in the legislative process in order to fulfill his sacred duty of self-government which was to hold his government accountable. It was not his personal opinion on any political issue that was so important. Why should it be when the individual was not a recognized source of authority? Rather, what counted was what God, the universally recognized authority, had to say about any issue or topic.

Thus the citizens who were not politicians could effectively govern themselves by directing their political representatives to obey God's directives in the Bible. Under the counsel of their clergy and by their own diligent studies and "searching" the Scriptures, they were acutely aware of God's directives on all freedom-related political issues.

The clergy throughout the colonies searched the Scriptures and taught the people what God said about virtually every issue pertaining to their political freedoms. There were no Abandonment Theologists back then. They considered freedom in all of its dimensions to be *of* God and that all matters of freedom were therefore the business of the church. In fact, the British declared that it was a Scottish clergyman, Dr. John Witherspoon (later to become president of The College of New Jersey, now known as Princeton University) who was primarily responsible for the American Revolution.

But this was not the whole dimension of self-government. The equally important duty of the citizen was to govern *himself* personally according to God's moral laws, specifically the Ten Commandments.

James Madison, known as the "Chief Architect of the Constitution," reportedly said:

> We have staked the whole future of American civilization, not upon the power of government, far from it. We have staked the future of all of our political institutions upon the capacity of mankind for self-government; upon the capacity of each and all of us to govern ourselves, and to control ourselves, to sustain ourselves according to the Ten Commandments of God.[14]

Bear in mind the fact that Satan never rests. His objective is to destroy America by corrupting her citizens' adherence to God's moral laws, even their ability to recognize them, and to disengage her Christian citizens (the church) from involvement in political affairs (a characteristic of Abandonment Theology). We've all heard the propaganda: "You can't legislate morality." But that is precisely what all legislation is - *somebody's* concept of morality. For America the Bible is the seat and standard of morality. Morality is the business of the Christian and

the church. Therefore, all legislation is the business of
the church.

To reiterate, the second dimension of self-government is the commitment of the citizens to govern themselves personally according to the laws and moral codes
of the Bible. If they fail in this sacred duty, they will be
unable to constrain the resulting unchained corruption
in the government. That is to say, the Constitution itself
derives its great strength and freedom-yielding powers
from a Bible-believing, Bible-obeying, vigilant citizenry.

Founding Father Dr. (Reverend) John Witherspoon,
expressed it this way:

> Nothing is more certain than that widespread
> immorality and corruption of manners make a
> people ripe for destruction... Beyond a certain
> point even the best constitution will be ineffec-
> tual and slavery must ensue. On the other hand,
> when the morals of a nation are pure; when true
> religion [Christianity - ed.] and moral principles
> maintain their vigor, the attempts of the most
> powerful enemies to oppress them are com-
> monly baffled and disappointed. God grant that
> in America true religion and civil liberty may be
> inseparable.[15]

Witherspoon also said:

> In free states where people have the supreme
> power in their own hands and must be consulted
> on all great matters, if there be a general corrup-
> tion of morals, there can be nothing but confu-
> sion. So true is this that civil liberty cannot long
> be preserved without virtue.[16]

The Founding Fathers designed our Bible-based
republic to be directly dependent upon the virtue of its

citizens and their ability to (1) govern themselves personally according to the moral codes of the Bible, especially the Ten Commandments of God; (2) be learned in the Scriptures so that with maximum authority and vigilance they could and would govern their political representatives by holding them accountable before God and the Bible. To that end the duty of the citizen was and is to elect righteous, God-fearing men to office.

> *Freedom is not free. Its beneficiaries carry with them enormous responsibilities to America and to posterity.*

Freedom is not free. Its beneficiaries carry with them enormous responsibilities to America and to posterity.

The way our republic was designed, the politicians at every level including the President are accountable through a Constitutional process to the citizens who must in turn, to be effective, govern themselves in the two ways cited above.

Ultimately, it all comes down to this: God is the Grantor of our freedoms. Everybody - our Congress, our political representatives, the citizens themselves - must obey God in the manner He sets forth in the Bible. If they do, America will remain free and invincible. To the extent that we abandon God, He will abandon us.

The Fathers gave us a good start. In 1831, years after the Constitution was ratified, the noted French statesman, historian and social philosopher Alexis deTocqueville traveled to America to discover the source of her vast commerce and boundless liberties. He concluded:

Not until I went to the churches of America and heard her pulpits flame with righteousness did I understand the secret of her genius and power... The Americans combine the notion of Christianity and liberty so intimately in their minds, that

it is impossible to make them conceive of one
without the other.[17]

In 1867 the *North American Review*, having witnessed our republic in action for nearly eighty years and
having seen the blessings and inspiration which flowed
out of her to the world, reported:

> The American government and the Constitu-
> tion is the most precious possession which the
> world holds, or which the future can inherit.
> This is true - true because the American system
> is the political expression of Christian ideas.[18]

Those Christian ideas equate to one thing: the freedom
that results from effective Bible-based self-government.

Despotisms, governments founded on Marxist/
Leninist communism, Nazism, etc. maximize government control over their citizens and minimize or eliminate entirely their rights to self-government. Our American Constitution, by contrast, is a government of "We the
People." The Constitution does not give the people their
rights or tell them what they can do. It cannot because
God does that in the Bible.

However, the Bill of Rights, amendments one through
ten of the Constitution, outlines those rights that God
already provides. The Bill of Rights was not a grant to the
people by the new government. It was a condition under
which the Constitution was signed which said, in effect,
to the government: Stay out of these areas. You do not
grant rights. God does. The Constitution operates to
secure them.

The Constitution establishes limits on the power of
the federal government and determines its relationship
with individual states. As the powers of government are
limited, our freedoms are maximized and so are our
responsibilities as self-governing citizens.

The Christian faith upon which our Declaration of Independence and Constitution were founded is a faith of resolve, commitment and personal responsibility to the God of the Old and New Testaments - to Christ Himself. Tough love is its centerpiece. This faith can triumph over the worst tyrants, carry the torch of freedom to the world and pour out blessings to all who live by it. But Christ demands our total commitment and loyalty by our vigilant and disciplined self-government. He has given us that opportunity through our American Constitutional Republic.

Democracy or Republic?

A pure democracy is unstable and by its essence cruel, enslaving and increasingly barbaric because it is founded upon the laws of fallen man.

Our American Constitutional Republic is stable and life-giving to individual citizens but a terror to despots. It is founded upon the righteous laws of God and the willingness of the citizens to live by them.

Did you know that the most intolerant person who ever walked on planet earth was Jesus Christ? Never once did He compromise with evil. He confronted it. His mission was to ...*destroy the works of the devil* (I John 3:8), never to compromise with them. The messages and examples of Christ are clear: confront evil and win. Lower your vigilance, attempt to compromise with it and, like inviting into your body just a little bit of malignant cancer, you (or your country) will ultimately die. With God it's all or nothing, total loyalty and commitment or no commitment at all.

William Penn, founder of Pennsylvania, summed it all up:

Those who will not be governed by God will be ruled by tyrants.[19]

"Governed by God" is our American Constitutional Republic, founded upon His moral and civil laws of righteousness. "Ruled by tyrants" is democracy founded upon the rule and laws of evil, of fallen man.

Authors or Expositors?

None of the Fathers, including the Reverend John Witherspoon, John Adams, John Jay, James Madison, Thomas Jefferson, John Quincy Adams, Alexander Hamilton or any others, claimed authorship of any ordinance or principle of the new American government. Rather, like John Calvin, their highest claim was that of "expositor" of the Word of God. When a Father in his diligent search of the Scriptures discovered a moral code, civil law or principle such as the separation of powers, it was submitted to Congress for consideration and adoption. The strength and power of our new republic must derive from truth - from the Word of God. Any lesser authority would contaminate the Godly foundation of the government.

Freedom is not a secular concept. Its essence is Spiritual. Had any of the Fathers attempted to interject the secular ideas of fallen man into the Divine structure of God's government, he would likely have been abruptly confronted or recalled by the state he represented. It was in this way that three million colonists and their political representatives were bound together in an invincible solidarity of focused purpose and commitment.

Christ taught the primacy of the spirit and the worth and dignity of the individual. He lifted up every man as a special creation made "in the image of God." For the first time in history a government was formed for the purpose of freeing the individual from his bondage and sufferings under tyrants and despots and for protecting his freedoms. This was precisely the fulfillment of Christ's first sermon in which He delivered His mission statement:

> *The Spirit of the Lord... hath anointed me ... to preach deliverance to the captives . . . to set at liberty them that are bruised* [persecuted, oppressed - ed.] (Luke 4:18).

If we are to save America's freedoms, it is vitally important that we know more about Christ as the true Author of those freedoms and our civil liberties. Who was, and is, He? Was He just the greatest of the teachers of moral codes and life principles, perhaps the greatest of the prophets? Whom did He proclaim *Himself* to be? Why was America born of Him and of none of the other prophets or religions? Could America have been founded on another religion?

Christianity as America's Religion

Jesus Christ brought to America's citizens undreamed-of political freedoms and such innumerable personal blessings that historians declared our Declaration of Independence and Constitutional Republic to be a "miracle."

Yet today it is widely taught that "all religions are basically the same," that their prophets teach the same moral and legal codes. But *are* they the same? Except for similar moral codes, can any "religion" be equated to Christianity? Why haven't they produced declarations of independence and constitutions which exalt and protect the individual, declaring that he is created in the image of God and has a Divine right to be free?

What's the difference? Why and how does Christianity liberate men from the bondage of sin, corruption and political tyranny while in historical and contemporary contrast, other religions, which we are incorrectly told are basically the same, tend to subordinate the individual to harsh systems of freedom-denying legalism or worse? The difference lies in the *person* of Christ.

> Biblical Christianity is absolutely unique in the nature of its central personage and founder, Jesus Christ. There is none other like Him in all history or even in all literature. Some writers, of course, presume to place Christ as merely one in a list of great religious leaders, but this is absurd. He stands in *contrast* to all others, not in line with them, not even at the head of the line.[20] (For more, see Appendix A.)

The Depth of Our Heritage

What, precisely, was the extent and depth of the Christian heritage left to us by the Founding Fathers? The United States Supreme Court spelled it out in 1892 in the case of *Church of the Holy Trinity v. United States:*

> Our laws and our institutions must necessarily be based upon and embody the teachings of The Redeemer of mankind. It is impossible that it should be otherwise; and in this sense and to this extent our civilization and our institutions are emphatically Christian... This is a religious people. This is historically true. From the discovery of this continent to the present hour, there is a single voice making this affirmation... we find everywhere a clear recognition of the same truth... These, and many other matters which might be noticed, add a volume of unofficial declarations to the mass of organic utterances that this is a Christian nation.[21]

What about the actual personal faith of the Fathers? Was Thomas Jefferson a Christian? What about Benjamin Franklin? How about other key Fathers such as George Washington, James Madison, John Jay, Alexander Hamilton, John Quincy Adams, John Adams, John Witherspoon, Patrick Henry?

Did you know that while in Philadelphia, Jefferson, a supposed deist, attended Christ Church along with Benjamin Franklin and George Washington, and in Williamsburg they attended the Bruton Parish Church? Speaking of the Bible and his faith, Jefferson stated:

> ... it is a document in proof that I am a real Christian; that is to say, a disciple of the doctrines of Jesus.[22]

The evidence speaks as loudly as the words. Few men did more for the advancement of the Christian faith than did Jefferson after he became President of the United States.

The Founding Fathers - Their Credentials and Faith

The Founding Fathers were clergymen, statesmen, educators, lawyers, physicians and highly successful businessmen. In contrast to what we often hear and read, they were overwhelmingly committed Christians. Those few not affiliated with a denomination left no doubt that they held a Christian Worldview.

The following is a brief profile of several of the best-known Fathers. It is only symbolic of the volumes which have been written on their Christian lives and convictions.

GEORGE WASHINGTON (1732-1799) was the first president of the United States and Commander in Chief of the Continental Army during the Revolutionary War.

Was George Washington, the "Father of our Country," a Christian? If so, to what extent? The answer to that question sets the stage for the heritage which all of us enjoy today. How outspoken was Washington to others about his faith?

Much has been written about Washington's Christian convictions - convictions so conspicuous that they ruled both his personal and military life as well as his public life as President of the United States. When he took the oath of office as our first President, he leaned over and kissed the Bible, which was opened to his favorite Book, Deuteronomy 28. His first and second Inaugural Addresses and National Thanksgiving Proclamation were permeated by references to God, the "Ruler of nations," the "Author of our blessings," and he spoke of His "Divine interposition" in the struggles of our nation.

He led his troops before and after battles in prayers of anticipation and thanksgiving. In fact, it is difficult to discover a publication of his in which he did not gratefully acknowledge or appeal to "Divine Providence." Washington considered America's victory over Great Britain to be nothing less than a miracle, and he constantly implored the citizens to be ever-mindful of that fact.

But what about Washington's private convictions? Was he truly a Christian - one who accepted Jesus Christ as his personal Savior? Beginning at a young age, Washington kept a personal prayer diary in which he wrote his prayers every day. Consider just a few excerpts:

Accept me for the merits of Thy Son Jesus Christ.[23]

From another diary entry:

> ...increase my faith, and direct me to the true object, Jesus Christ the Way, the Truth and the Life, bless, O Lord, all the people of this land, from the highest to the lowest, particularly those whom Thou hast appointed to rule us in church and state.[24]

Another excerpt:

> ...Direct my thoughts, words and work, wash away my sins in the immaculate Blood of the Lamb, and purge my heart by Thy Holy Spirit... Daily frame me more and more unto the likeness of Thy Son, Jesus Christ, that living in Thy fear, and dying in Thy favor, I may in Thy appointed time attain the resurrection of the just unto eternal life. Bless my family, friends and kindred, and unite us all in praising and glorifying Thee in all our works.[25]

Nearly all of the Fathers possessed the same Christian zeal and depth of faith as that of Washington.

JAMES MADISON (1751-1836), known as the "Chief Architect of the Constitution," was the fourth President of the United States, from 1809 till 1817. He was a member of the first United States Congress and was the original author and promoter of the Bill of Rights, of which he made religious freedom the first item.

He was appointed by President Thomas Jefferson as U.S. Secretary of State where he engineered the Louisiana Purchase of 1803. He was acting President and Commander in Chief during the War of 1812 and had to flee the White House before it was captured and burned by the British.

James Madison was an instrumental member of the Constitutional Convention, speaking 161 times - more than any other Founder except Governeur Morris. His records of the debates in the Constitutional Convention are the most accurate and detailed that exist.

In addition to being a lawyer and planter, Madison was a member of the House of Delegates. As a Virginia legislator he helped write the Constitution of Virginia and authored 29 of the 85 *Federalist* papers, which argued successfully in favor of the ratification of the Constitution.

It was James Madison who made the motion, seconded by Roger Sherman, that Benjamin Franklin's famous appeal for prayer at the Constitutional Convention be enacted.

Home-schooled as a child, Madison attended Princeton University under the direction of Reverend John Witherspoon, one of the nation's premier theologians and legal scholars. The college at one time declared, "Cursed be all learning that is contrary to the cross of Christ."

James Madison, on June 20, 1785, wrote in regard to the relationship between religion and civil government:

Religion [is] the basis and Foundation of Government.[26]

JOHN WITHERSPOON (1723-1794), a signer of the Declaration of Independence, was a member of the Continental Congress who served on over 100 congressional committees. An American revolutionary patriot of Scottish birth, Witherspoon became a famous educator, clergyman and the president of Princeton College.

Princeton College, originally called The College of New Jersey, was founded in 1746 in Princeton, New Jersey by the Presbyterian Church. Its official motto was: "Under God's Power She Flourishes."

Reverend John Witherspoon's emphasis of Biblical

principles having an impact on government was tremendously felt in the colonies during the foundation of America. His influence continued through his students, including one President, one Vice-President, three Supreme Court justices, ten cabinet members, twelve governors, twenty-one senators, thirty-nine representatives as well as numerous delegates to the Constitutional Convention and state leaders. His students included leaders such as Gunning Bedford of Delaware, David Brearly of New Jersey and James Madison, who served eight years as Secretary of State and eight years as President.

John Witherspoon stated:

It is in the man of piety and inward principle, that we may expect to find the uncorrupted patriot, the useful citizen, and the invincible soldier - God grant that in America true religion and civil liberty may be inseparable and that the unjust attempts to destroy the one, may in the issue tend to the support and establishment of both.[27]

BENJAMIN FRANKLIN was one of America's most instrumental statesman. He founded the University of Pennsylvania. He was governor of Pennsylvania and signed the Declaration of Independence, the Articles of Confederation and the Constitution. It was Franklin who broke the deteriorating stalemate of the Constitutional Convention of 1787 held in the State House in Philadelphia when he stood and delivered a Christian oration that captivated the hearts of all in attendance.

I have lived, Sir, a long time; and the longer I live the more convincing proofs I see of this Truth, that God governs in the affairs of men! And if a sparrow cannot fall to the ground without His notice, is it probable that an empire can rise without His aid?[28]

Were these the words of a deist? Had the inspired Franklin been unable to call forth with mastery, eloquence and power his deep knowledge and love of the Scriptures, historians contend that the Constitutional Convention would have dissolved. There would have been no Constitution, and America would have slipped back under the tyranny of King George of England.

Today we often hear Franklin accused of being a deist. He himself admits that as a young man he went through a period of intense searching. Like Jefferson, Franklin rejected the institutionalized church, but both were scholars of the Scriptures.

A Final Thought

If this brief overview of our heritage seems new to you, don't feel alone. Extensive research by eminently qualified contemporary historians proves that it's no accident. An attorney friend who minored in American History at one of America's top universities, after reading the manuscript of *Abandonment Theology* commented, "At first I was shocked and upset. On my second reading it made me mad... mad at my teachers and my professors, mad at my ministers, because I suddenly realized that I had been cheated out of one of the most priceless aspects of an education - a knowledge of my sacred heritage as an American citizen."

Let's next consider some ways in which America's foundations have been and are being destroyed.

CHAPTER TWO

THE DECLINE BEGINS:
A FORMULA FOR DESCENT

If the foundations be destroyed,
what can the righteous do?
Psalm 11:3

The "Wall of Separation"

Founder John Adams stressed it time and again: there has never been a time in history when men rose to power and subsequently liberated their fellow man. Those in power have eventually become oppressors. For one to trust in his fellow man and hope for the best would be an act of folly and exceedingly dangerous to liberty. The maxim of Proverbs 29:2 holds true: *When the righteous are in authority, the people rejoice: but when the wicked beareth rule, the people mourn.*

The responsibility of "We the People," the citizens of America, to ensure that the righteous are in authority has been dangerously hampered by the introduction of a single concept: the "wall of separation" between church and state.

In 1947 Justice of the U.S. Supreme Court Hugo Black *(Everson v. Board of Education)* declared that such a wall must exist between the church and the state. He had taken out of context an expression from one of Thomas Jefferson's letters, a letter to the Danbury Baptist Association, written years after the First Amendment had been ratified.[29] The Court apparently ignored

39

the true notion of Jefferson's "wall" illustration - that a wall must exist to forbid the government from intruding into the affairs of the church. Justice Black, *with no precedent,* decided that the reverse was also necessary - that the church must not be involved with the affairs of state. Jefferson's "wall" was a one-way wall; the Court's was a two-way wall. In fact, there is no mention of the words "church" or "separation" in the First Amendment or in the body of the Constitution, and the word "state" is used only in reference to states' rights, not the separation issue.

That landmark Supreme Court decision was strictly a political one, not based on cases establishing precedents. The very essence of our Christian-based republic is a citizen's responsibility to choose righteous political representatives coupled with his or her obligation to watch over them and make sure they guard our freedoms. The government was designed to be the servant of the citizens. Any notion of a "wall" limiting the church's direct influence in the legislative or moral affairs of political representatives or institutions preempts the ability of a citizen to do his sacred duty. That twist of words - from the time of the Everson case forward - would allow and in fact invite our political representatives and the Supreme Court itself in future cases to rule according to their "fallen human nature."

The Foundation Erodes

Founding Father Reverend John Witherspoon recognized that any nation's strength depends on its spiritual foundation.

In free states where people have the supreme power in their own hands and must be consulted on all great matters, if there be a general corruption of morals, there can be nothing but confusion. So true is this, that civil liberty cannot long be preserved without virtue.... Nothing is more certain than that widespread immorality and corruption of manners make a people ripe for destruction.... Beyond a certain point even the best constitution will be ineffectual and slavery must ensue. On the other hand, when the morals of a nation are pure, when true religion and moral principles maintain their vigor, the attempts of the most powerful enemies to oppress them are commonly baffled and disappointed. God grant that in America true religion and civil liberty may be inseparable.[30]

Looking across time, Witherspoon concluded:

I look upon the cause of America to be a matter of truly inexpressible importance. The state of the human race across much of the globe for ages to come depends upon it.[31]

Is America still the lighthouse for the "state of the human race" as Witherspoon described? Let's compare the heritage given us by our Founding Fathers with what it is becoming today. America was founded upon this premise:

There is but one law for all, namely, that law which governs all law, the law of our Creator, the law of humanity, justice, equity - the law of nature and of nations.[32]

Moral Relativism

One telling indication of America's spiritual state is evident in the widespread acceptance and propagation of moral relativism. The principle of eternal absolutes has been eroding into broad tolerance, even of recognized evils.

> Ethical relativism is the belief that no absolute moral code exists, and therefore man must adjust his ethical standards in each situation according to his own judgment.[33]

> By rejecting any kind of purpose behind the existence of a code of ethics, one necessarily finds himself rejecting any code that may exist outside of man. This done, all ethics are relative to man's interpretation of them in any given situation.[34]

This anti-God cancer of relative moral standards has had an impact on all of life in America as it planted its roots deeply in our schools and educational system. In the early 1920s Dr. John Dewey, professor at Columbia University and a founder of the American Humanist Association, introduced a concept termed "Progressive Education" which spread throughout our nation's public school system. He held that:

> There is no God and there is no soul. Hence, there are no needs for the props of traditional religion. With dogma and creed excluded, then immutable truth is also dead and buried. There is no room for fixed, natural law or moral absolutes.[35]

Contemporary theologian Dr. D. James Kennedy observed the consequences of Dewey's progressive education:

> Little wonder that the Dewey-ite secular humanists who have led education in this country for the past 50 years have helped to produce a

veritable slime pit of immorality, drug addiction, sexual perversion, permissiveness, and diseases of every sort.... Effects that, according to eminent educator, Professor Jacques Barzun, have resulted in turning the once proud and efficient public school system of the United States "into a wasteland where violence and vice share the times with ignorance and idleness."[36]

The youth of America are our sacred trust from God. They are our future. What have the churches been doing during this protracted assault upon the minds and spirits of America's young people?

The Chain of Events

Outlawing Prayer: In the 1962 U. S. Supreme Court case of *Engel v. Vitale,* the Court declared "unconstitutional" a strictly voluntary, non-denominational school prayer composed by the New York Board of Regents. This, as the Chief Justice of the New York Court of Appeals declared, was "in defiance of all American history."[37] Not a single precedent was cited by the court.

A remnant of voices cried out in protest from the wilderness. However, a majority of undiscerning Christian citizenry quietly watched as the sword stabbed into the heart of America's heritage and future. Why did this happen? Where were the clergy? The Abandonment Clergy were refusing to "become involved" in what they called a "political issue" when it was most obviously a religious or Biblical issue.

Outlawing Bible Reading: But there was more to come. On June 17, 1963 the Supreme Court recertified its intent in the cases of *School District of Abington Township v. Schempp* and *Murray v. Curlett.* In a Baltimore suit instigated by avowed atheist Madelyn Murray O'Hair, the justices ruled it was unconstitutional for a state to have portions of the Bible recited in schools, having determined that this was an "establishment of religion." Justice Potter Stewart, the lone dissenting vote, said that the ruling had not led to true neutrality with respect to religion but rather to the "establishment of a religion of secularism."[38]

Two days after the "establishment of secularism," the *Wall Street Journal* commented that atheism was now "the one belief to which the state's power will extend its protection."[39] In light of this case some states banned all prayers and Bible reading. A lower court even decreed *(Stein v. Oshinsky)* that kindergarten children could not pray, "God is great, God is good, and we thank Him for our food. Amen."[40]

Outlawing the Ten Commandments: Next to be stricken from schools were the Ten Commandments, the very pillars of liberty and social structure upon which our American Constitutional Republic is founded. *Honor thy father and thy mother; Thou shalt not kill; Thou shalt not commit adultery; Thou shalt not steal; Thou shalt not bear false witness;... Thou shalt not covet,* etc. (Ex. 20:12-17). All were upended in the 1980 Supreme Court ruling in *Stone v. Graham.* The Court found that it is "unconstitutional for the Ten Commandments to hang on the walls of a classroom, since students might be led to read them, meditate upon them, respect them, or obey them."[41] Once again the American people responded with a whimper.

James Madison, "Chief Architect of the Constitution," probably would have thrown a fit. He reportedly said:

> We have staked the whole future of American civilization not on the power of government. Far from it! We have staked the future of all of our political institutions upon the capacity . . . of each and all of us to govern ourselves . . . according to the Ten Commandments of God.[42]

Although Madison is credited with making that particular statement, all of the Fathers in their speeches, writings, even engravings in the granite and interior of the Federal buildings in Washington, D.C. said the same thing. Their worldview was unanimously Christian, and the Ten Commandments formed the pillars upon which their faith and all Constitutional civil law rested.

Some Statistical Evidence

The Scriptures tell us that God is patient and merciful but that He will not be mocked (See Gal. 6:7). He draws the line, and when our neglect of His laws of liberty and of our sacred trust - our children - passes a certain point, He will give harsh notice that our nation is heading toward a loss of liberty and collapse.

Many have speculated, based upon statistical and observable evidence, that God reached His limit in 1962 when the U.S. Supreme Court, in effect, outlawed prayer and Bible reading in our nation's schools and reaffirmed His limit in 1980 when the posting of the Ten Commandments in the classroom was declared unconstitutional.

It would appear that in 1962, when God saw the neglect and impotence of the clergy and other citizens, barring a remnant "crying in the wilderness," He must have said in effect, "You've crossed the line," and He removed His protective hand from our country.

On the following pages, Figures 2 through 6, provided by one of our nation's foremost authorities on these matters, David Barton, offer dramatic evidence as to what happened as a result. There are some who speculate that God had nothing to do with it, that a whole complex of events suddenly precipitated in a simultaneous eruption having an impact on many dimensions of social life. That might be true, but it seems far more logical that God Himself delivered the warning because that explanation is in perfect harmony with the Scriptures. The key term is *simultaneous*. The figures are keyed to the year 1962.

Declining Scholastic Aptitude Test Scores

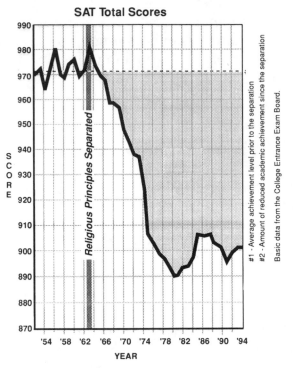

Courtesy of David Barton, WallBuilders, Inc., Aledo, TX[43]

Figure 2. Scholastic Aptitude Test Score Decline

Figure 2 shows the drastic decline of Scholastic Aptitude Test (SAT) scores since 1962. Christ instructs us to walk the highest moral road, to diligently seek excellence in all things, using the Word of God as the foundation of wisdom and upon which all true knowledge is built. Life must have its purpose. The wellspring of happiness and true achievement which brings purpose and calls for excellence, that makes life worth living, is the love of God, the knowledge of Him and our obedience to His precepts of truth and liberty. When the U.S. Supreme Court outlawed God in the public schools, the foundation of character and of America's heritage went with Him. Thus the SAT scores plunged.

Violent Crimes Escalate

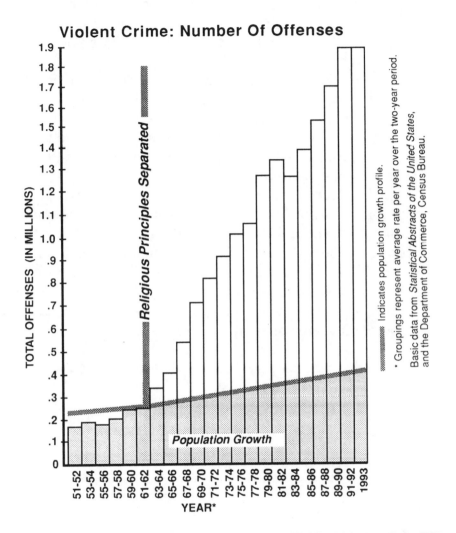

Figure 3. The Rise of Violent Crime

Figure 3 illustrates the crime wave that has been escalating since 1962. Why are so many people afraid to go out for a walk at night? It didn't used to be that way. Killings, muggings, rapes, sadistic mass murders - every day the papers are filled with stories. Handguns are being bought in record numbers for self-defense. The value of life itself seems to have plummeted. Following the outlawing of God in the public schools, violent crime exploded. Why?

The answer is obvious. Christ taught the primacy of the spirit and the worth and dignity of the individual. These were His messages that students learned in their daily Bible reading in the schools. Remove God, and the law of the jungle, which is governed by man's fallen nature, fills the vacuum.

The Founding Fathers wrote that if obedience to God were removed from national life, a wave of crime would be unleashed which would eventually bankrupt federal and state treasuries in their frantic attempts to control it. Prayer and Bible reading and posting the Ten Commandments have been, in effect, outlawed in America's public schools. Our Founders' warnings have been ignored, and we are reaping the consequences of disobedience.

The Moral Standard Collapses

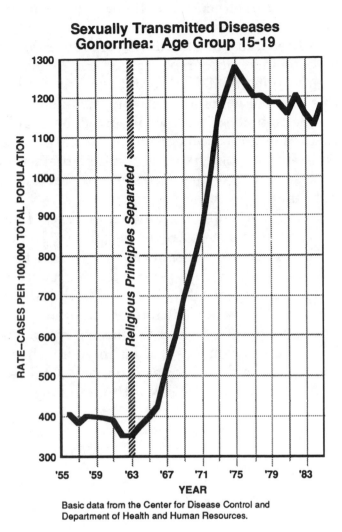

Basic data from the Center for Disease Control and
Department of Health and Human Resources.

Courtesy of David Barton, WallBuilders, Inc. Aledo, TX[45]

Figure 4. The Rise of Sexually Transmitted Diseases

Figure 4 shows the rise of sexually transmitted
diseases since 1962 and gives substance to the expression, "Today, sex out of wedlock is more dangerous than
Russian Roulette." In fact, if one or both of the partners

in the marriage were sexually active prior to marriage, there is a high likelihood that he or she is carrying a potentially deadly sexual disease.

Gonorrhea and a multitude of sexually transmitted diseases have suddenly climbed to epidemic levels. AIDS, for example, unheard of until recent years, is deadly and incurable. Billions of dollars are being spent on research for cures. Sex outside of wedlock is rooted in the godless, humanistic "feel good" social philosophy, the philosophy that represents a quick fix with instant satisfaction for natural desires but denies God's moral framework in their fulfillment.

How many would-be beautiful marriages, families and children have been destroyed because God's rules of life and happiness were disobeyed? In 1962, when the Abandonment Clergy did not protest the Supreme Court's unprecedented decision which resulted in the outlawing of God in the schools (and ultimately in public institutions), obedience to God's moral codes significantly diminished. The consequences, often including horrible, agonizing death, afflicted great numbers of those who broke God's laws governing sex within marriage.

Unwed Pregnancies Have Skyrocketed

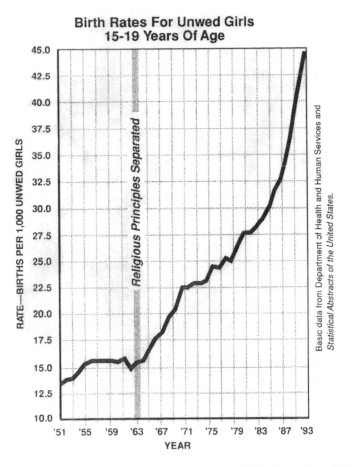

Courtesy of David Barton, WallBuilders, Inc. Aledo, TX[46]

Figure 5. The Rise of Pregnancies in Unwed Girls

Pregnancies in unwed girls have increased dramatically since 1962, showing that when we removed God, high moral purpose went with Him. The number of children born outside of marriage has skyrocketed, and the abortion mills do an ever greater and more profitable business. The lives of the young mothers are often traumatized for years while the beauty and treasures of motherhood are desecrated. God's purpose is defeated. The nation is weakened. God will not be mocked.

Divorce Rates and the Stability of the Nation

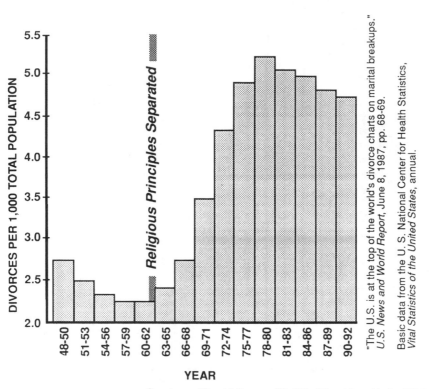

Courtesy of David Barton, WallBuilders, Inc. Aledo, TX[47]

Figure 6. The Increasing Divorce Rate

"A family that prays together, stays together." Just about everybody has heard that truism. Figure 6 shows what happened to marriages when God's influence was removed from young lives.

The bedrock of America's spiritual, political and economic strength, of her greatness as a nation, is the God-centered family institution. Children are a sacred trust from God to their parents in the sanctity of their home. (See Deut. 6:6,7.)

When God does not stand in the center of the lives of a married couple or of a family, the door is opened to Satan and his devastation. To destroy the family is to destroy our God-given nation. There is only one answer to marriages in trouble, and it is *not* secular or humanistic social counseling. As in the schools, there is no substitute for God - the Source and fountainhead of love, strength, happiness and purpose.

I AM MUCH AFRAID THAT SCHOOLS WILL PROVE TO BE GREAT GATES OF HELL UNLESS THEY DILIGENTLY LABOR IN EXPLAINING THE HOLY SCRIPTURES, ENGRAVING THEM IN THE HEARTS OF YOUTH.
I ADVISE NO ONE TO PLACE HIS CHILD WHERE THE SCRIPTURES DO NOT REIGN PARAMOUNT.
EVERY INSTITUTION IN WHICH MEN ARE NOT INCREASINGLY OCCUPIED WITH THE WORD OF GOD MUST BECOME CORRUPT.

MARTIN LUTHER

The consequences of removing God from the schools were predictable. Martin Luther, the Father of the Protestant Reformation instigated in the sixteenth century, foresaw what would happen if God was abandoned in the classroom.

America's Founding Fathers felt so strongly about the issue that in the Northwest Ordinance, they required territories which applied for statehood to prove that their educational system was anchored in the Bible.

The Abandonment Clergy need to come off their reservations, get into the battle, and lead their people in taking on the Supreme Court directly and through their elected representatives. We need to give those gallant organizations already on the front lines the support they need to win decisive victories and get God back into the schools according to the heritage of our country.

Military Vulnerability and the Outlawing of God

Although Figures 2 through 6 concern the sudden across-the-board loss of stable social life following the Supreme Court's decisions regarding prayer and Bible reading in America's schools, there is one more consideration - the impact upon America's military defenses. The lesson of history is that when nations turn their backs on God, all of life deteriorates, confusion sets in as a consequence of a lack of Spiritual discernment, and military vulnerability results. Suddenly, when it is too late, once free people find themselves defenseless before invading armies. Is that what is happening to America?

The next chapter examines America's present military vulnerability and some of her historic positions on foreign policy that have led to her critically weakened military strength.

CHAPTER THREE

MILITARY VULNERABILITY

For if the trumpet give an uncertain sound,
who shall prepare himself to the battle?
I Corinthians 14:8

Spiritual Blindness and America's Military Disarmament

What tumultuous event or series of events could bring upon a nation of free people such blindness or incomprehension that they would passively allow their vital military defenses to be *unilaterally* disarmed in a world of increasingly formidable enemies? This chapter examines that question.

America has long been engaged in a policy of unilateral military disarmament. In fact, America's lack of military capability was so advanced by 1980 that former Secretary of State Dr. Henry A. Kissinger went on record with the following testimony to Congress:

> We have placed ourselves at a significant disadvantage, militarily... It is the consequence of unilateral decisions extending over a decade and a half, of a strategic doctrine adopted in the 60s, and of the choices of the present administration. All these actions were unilateral, hence avoidable. Rarely in history has a nation so passively accepted such a radical change in the military balance.[48]

When a people who have long enjoyed the blessings of God's liberty become contemptuous of the Author of that liberty, it is not unreasonable to anticipate that God will reach the end of His patience and withdraw His protective hand. Chapter Two examined America's moral decline after the Supreme Court decision regarding prayer and Bible reading in the schools. Her Christians, neutralized by the Abandonment Clergy, let it happen.

Could it be that a terrible Spiritual blindness followed in the wake of this blatant abandonment of God, rendering the people unable to divide truth from error? Were they therefore unable to discern what was happening militarily to our country, resulting in peril to our freedoms if such a policy was not stopped? Otherwise, how in such a volatile world of enemies sworn to our destruction could America's Christians abandon God's mandate of eternal vigilance? How could they accept our government's disarming "peace in our time" propaganda and its corresponding proposals that America subordinate her freedoms and independence to a tyrannical, godless United Nations leading to world government?

Throughout history tyrants such as Hitler, Mao Tse Tung, Stalin, Lenin, and Gorbachev in their lust for power have forsaken even their own people and reduced their lives to perpetual agony. In our century alone the mercilessness of unbridled "fallen man" to his fellow man has exceeded anything known in the long, cruel, bloody history of godless tyrannies. Those, such as evolutionists, who contend that man is improving and rising to a higher state, have only to observe the record of history.

Why, in view of this record of man's propensity toward power and cruelty, would our free nation consider lowering its guard as it has done against the injunctions of God in the Bible, entering instead into treaties in which it staked its vital security on the hoped-for good faith of such godless tyrants? Why would the clergy tolerate it? Why would they not sound the alarm, the "trumpet," loudly and clearly to the people instead of leading them in the illusion of "peace" to a most precarious fate?

The United Nations: Big Brother, Ruthless Master

As America turns her back on God, she is being ushered into a predictable fate under the godless UN New World Order, now commonly referred to as the "New Civilization." A deadly, global world citizenship outlook is gaining much favor especially among our young people. It is well-expressed by George Canning:

> A steady patriot of the world alone,
> The friend of every country but his own.[49]

It should greatly concern Americans that we are so close to relinquishing our sovereignty to the UN.

We're accustomed to a political system that has a solid basis for liberty: God, Himself. Our Declaration of Independence opens by affirming that all men are "endowed by their *Creator* with certain unalienable rights, among which are life, liberty, and the pursuit of happiness." The government designed by God is the people's *servant,* not their master, and the people are given authority over it.

In contrast the UN *does not even acknowledge God's existence* in the Charter's "Declaration of Human Rights." Any human rights to be preserved are those rights authorized and granted by the UN, not by God. Reason says that if a government can *grant* rights, it can also *withdraw* them. The United Nations is accountable only to itself, not to the people of the world.

Rights granted to men by other men should remind us of Proverbs 14:12 - *There is a way that seems right to a man, but its end is the way of death.* If the UN has no higher authority than itself, it can freely operate according to the cruelty of fallen human nature and man's rationale.

Placing the UN in this position of power could spell the end of America's sovereignty and freedom as we know it. Of course, a powerful UN world military force theoretically will be used to enforce "peace" in the world, but that same military force could reign down terror on a disarmed, helpless America.

The UN Declaration leads to slavery; the American Declaration leads to freedom. That difference must be urgently impressed upon our citizens. The dreamers who envision world peace as meaning only freedom from conflict must face reality, or the horrors described below may well become the reality in both their own and their children's lives.

It Won't Happen to Us, Right?

Americans have lived for so long in a land of milk and honey - prosperity, material wealth and luxuries, individual freedoms - that we have nearly forgotten of what barbarity man is capable. But the UN "peacekeeper" record of brutality to date speaks for itself. An example is the UN record of "murder, mayhem, rape and pillaging the Katanga province of the Congo in 1960."[50] What's to stop an all-powerful UN from inflicting the same upon America?

We think of battlefields and wars as the primary cause of violent death. Not so. Professor R. J. Rummel writes in *Lethal Politics* (his book of 20th century statistics about genocide and mass murder since 1900) that in this century three times more men, women and children have died at the hands of their own governments than in wars. Millions have died by torture, beatings, starvation, genocide and execution in the most merciless ways.

In Soviet Russia alone over 60 million experienced such deaths since the 1917 Revolution. One Soviet woman, when asked how it could have happened, said simply, "We turned our back on God."

According to Rummel's statistics, roughly three times more people have been put to death in purges, reigns of terror, and outright genocide than in actual wars. Rummel says this:

> I surveyed the extent of genocide and mass killing by governments since 1900. The results were shocking: according to these first figures - independent of war and other kinds of conflict - governments probably have murdered 119,400,000 people - Marxist governments about 95,200,000 of them. By comparison, the battle-killed in all foreign and domestic wars in this century total 35,700,000.[51]

Women, children, infants, elderly people - all were treated the same. They died during mass deportations to slave labor camps, often freezing in cattle cars. They died under cruel, barbaric conditions in the concentration camps. Millions of Ukrainians died of famine and mass executions at the hands of Nikita Khrushchev when Stalin was his master. Millions perished from beatings, torture and by every manner of bestial process under Stalin between 1936 and 1938 during "The Great Terror Period." In Cambodia half the population was destroyed in Marxist Pol Pot's "ethnic cleansing."

Rummel asserts that Mao Tse Tung in China brought over 20 million deaths. Christians and clergy were among those hunted down and murdered in the most heinous ways.

Germany's Hitler decreed to destroy every Jew in Europe and reportedly murdered six million of them before his blood purges, torture chambers and gas chambers were stopped by the allied forces.

According to Rummel's figures, the total number of citizens murdered by their own governments is more than "four times the battle dead (15,000,000) for all nations in the Second World War. Indeed, it exceeds the total deaths (35,654,000) from all this century's international, civil, guerilla and liberation wars, including Russia's civil war itself."[52]

If we were to go back in history and come forward through the Dark Ages (when people were totally ignorant of the Bible, and there was no advancement in science, culture, literature, etc.) and through the inquisitions and terror by despots, we would conclude that we in America have been blessed with our freedoms beyond any possible description. But will those blessings continue if we do not help ourselves?

Military Vulnerability

The figures in Chapter 2 concern the sudden, simultaneous, across-the-board disruption of stable social life in America which followed the Supreme Court's outlawing of prayer and Bible reading in our schools. However, there is another consideration - the impact upon America's military defenses.

Was it coincidental that an official program for the military disarming of the United States and her citizens was launched almost simultaneously with the 1962 Supreme Court decision? Again, we experienced no response from the clergy and near silence from the American people. Here's what happened.

On September 25, 1961, President John F. Kennedy presented to the United Nations General Assembly a disarmament proposal entitled "Freedom From War: The United States Program for General and Complete

Disarmament in a Peaceful World." Known as Department of State Publication 7277, this document states:

> The overall goal of the United States is ...a world which has achieved general and complete disarmament under effective international control; and a world in which adjustment to change takes place in accordance with the principles of the United Nations.[53]

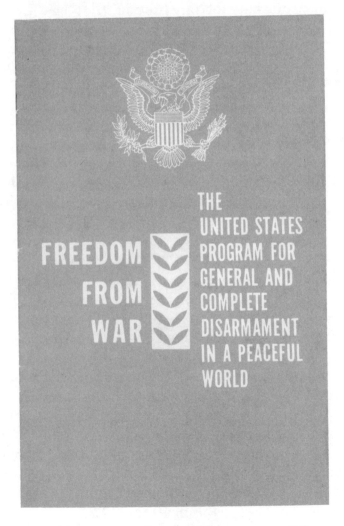

Figure 7. Cover of Department of State
Publication 7277

President Kennedy proposed to disarm the United States of her military defenses and fighting ability, and her citizens personally, in three phases. In the end America would be defenseless and non-existent as a free, sovereign nation, and she would be under the military and political dominance of the godless United Nations.

At the time of President Kennedy's speech the U.S.S.R. occupied one of the five permanent seats on the United Nations Security Council. That fact in itself made a farce and mockery of any notion that the United Nations was committed to world peace - by Western definition of the term. Why? Because according to their own statements confirmed by their record, the U.S.S.R. and Red China wanted power, not peace.

> *President Kennedy proposed to disarm the United States of her military defenses and fighting ability, and her citizens personally. In the end America would be defenseless and non-existent as a free, sovereign nation, and she would be under the military and political dominance of the godless United Nations.*

What's more, since the UN's founding in 1946, it has had six Undersecretaries for Political and Security Council Affairs, and all have been Communists. Today this office still controls all military functions of the UN "peace" forces.

President Kennedy's 1961 disarmament proposal took root. In April of 1962 he submitted another proposal to an 18-nation disarmament committee. It was entitled "Blueprint for the Peace Race: Outline of Basic Provisions of a Treaty on General and Complete Disarmament in a Peaceful World."[54] This new plan was simply a more detailed description of the proposals originally set forth in Department of State Publication 7277.

Did anybody outside of the government sound the

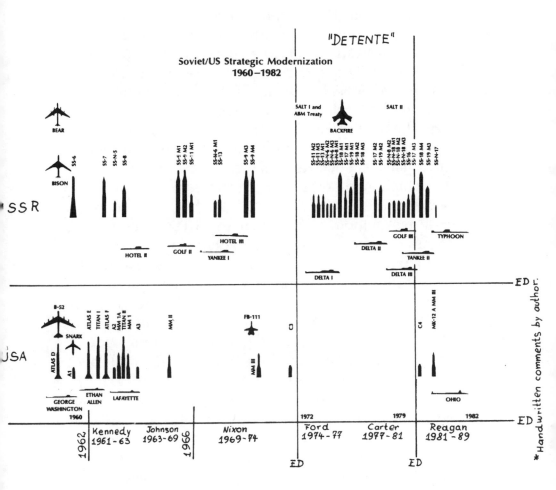

**Figure 8. Soviet Military Power 1990,
Department of Defense[55]**

Can America's unilateral military disarmament be blamed on any one
administration? It appears that weapons systems already in the
"pipeline" in 1962 (when God was shown the door in our public schools)
were completed, but then a power far greater than a political one seems
to have taken control.

alarm about 7277 to the unsuspecting American citizens? Yes. Copies of that infamous State Department document were obtained by evangelical preachers and reprinted by the hundreds of thousands and distributed to their followers. These fearless clergymen made radio broadcasts nationwide and exhausted every avenue for the exposure of the probable consequences to America's freedoms. The media branded them as "extremists" and "paranoid." But our government leaders were absorbed in fanciful policies such as "peaceful coexistence" and "detente" which by their essence were based upon trust and assumed the good intentions of those vowed to America's destruction. Observe in the Department of Defense chart, Figure 8, the unprecedented Soviet military production during the Brezhnev detente era and compare it to the United States under several presidents.

Figure 8 compares the U.S. and U.S.S.R. new weapons production for the period 1960 to 1982. Note that production nearly ceased in the U.S. after 1962 and prior to the Reagan Administration, but the U.S.S.R. accelerated a massive buildup which it accomplished under the U.S./U.S.S.R. pact known as "detente." In addition to all but ceasing production, "Beginning in 1961 the U.S. phased out 1,000 B-47 bombers; in 1970 our B-58 strategic bombers were deactivated; President Carter in 1977 cancelled the B-1 bomber which was to replace our obsolete B-52 bombers. The number of U.S. strategic missiles was frozen at the 1967 level."[56]

Scaling the bottom (U.S.) portion of Figure 8, it appears that shortly after 1962 in the wake of the Supreme Court decision a near freeze on U.S. modernization and new weapons production went into effect. Evidently, new weapons already planned and budgeted were completed, but U.S. production fell to zero during the latter part of the Nixon Administration ('69-'74) and stayed at zero during the Ford Administration ('74-'77) and the Carter Administration ('77-'81).

The American people were sold on the good intentions of the Soviets. Peace, friendship and trust culminated in the new "detente" relationship. In 1972 the United States entered into an anti-ballistic missile (ABM) treaty with the U.S.S.R. in which "both parties agreed not to test, construct or operate an anti-missile defense system."[57] America held rigidly to the treaty. The U.S.S.R. broke it and proceeded to develop highly sophisticated "first-strike" missile and defense systems. In 1973 Soviet Premier Brezhnev made the U.S.S.R.'s intentions clear: "By 1985, we will be able to extend our will wherever we wish."[58]

By 1980 America's military crisis was so acute that presidential contender Ronald Reagan made a major election issue of it. On May 29, 1980 all the members of the Joint Chiefs of Staff and General David Jones,

Former head of the DIA, the late General Daniel Graham, recognizing the increasing dangers to America from a Soviet ICBM first-strike, called together an association of our nation's top scientists and asked them to devise a purely defensive, non-nuclear system for defending our cities against a surprise missile attack.

Chairman, went together as a body to testify to Congress' House Armed Services Committee that the Administration's budget was not adequate to meet our defense needs. Chairman of the Investigations Subcommittee, Sam Stratton, said, "This was the first time in history that the Joint Chiefs had testified as a body in opposition to an Administration position."[59]

In March, 1981 President Reagan announced a five-year budget for a crash defense buildup. By 1988, "Every penny of the Reagan defense buildup announced in March, 1981, has been deleted plus an additional cut of $38 billion."[60]

Former head of the Defense Intelligence Agency (DIA), the late General Daniel Graham, recognizing the increasing dangers to America from a Soviet ICBM first-strike, called together an association of our nation's top scientists and asked them to devise a purely defensive, non-nuclear system for defending our cities against a surprise missile attack. They did, and it became known as the Strategic Defense Initiative (SDI).

In brief it consisted of super-fast kinetic energy rockets (Space-Based Interceptors (SBIs)) launched from satellites, which could attack and destroy missiles any-where in the world after leaving their launch sites. For example, an SS-18 ICBM, launched from Russia, Red China, N. Korea, Iran or any other such country, carrying ten nuclear warheads targeted on ten different American cities would be detected upon launch. Its trajectory would be calculated, and an SBI rocket would be fired from a satellite to intercept and destroy it as it entered its "boost" stage or in other stages thereafter. In 1983 President Reagan disclosed this revolutionary "inexpensive" defense system to the American public by television. The media mockingly called it "Star Wars."

Since then no effort has been spared in certain congressional circles to prevent the actual development and deployment of SDI. "What is being challenged today,...[is] the Clinton Administration's policy of intentionally leaving American cities and territory open to missile attack."[61]

Most Americans have no idea that our country is undefended. This policy of defenselessness is referred to by The Heritage Foundation as: "...this sorry legacy of intentionally keeping the United States of America vulnerable to missile attack."[62]

On May 14, 1993 *The Orlando Sentinel* carried headlines, "Aspin writes 'Star Wars' obituary." The story opened:

Ten years and $30 billion after President Reagan declared his vision of a leakproof shield against

Soviet nuclear attack, the "Star Wars" program is officially dead.

[Defense Secretary Les Aspin told a news conference at the Pentagon], "Today we are here to observe another point of passage, which is the end of the "Star Wars" era.[63]

It is so hard to believe that America has no defense against attacking ballistic missiles which may carry nuclear, chemical or biological warheads, that it is appropriate to quote the highest source - Secretary of Defense William Perry. Secretary Perry testified in early March, 1996 before a congressional committee on Ballistic Missile Defenses (BMD):

We have no capability to shoot down any ballistic missiles fired at the United States.[64]

It is inconceivable that the American people, particularly America's Christians, would have tolerated such a policy as President Kennedy's planned disarmament of America unless they were

We have no capability to shoot down any ballistic missiles fired at the United States.

themselves suffering from Spiritual blindness or a nearly total abdication of their sacred duties as citizens to monitor all political affairs. Was it, and *is* it, a blindness induced by God upon a nation that has turned its back on Him?

How did the disbanding of our defenses happen, step-by-step, without protest except from an ignored remnant of alarmed patriots? Perhaps the next section, "Soviet Smoke and America's Military Crisis," will help you understand.

Soviet Smoke and America's Military Crisis

Geopolitical historians explain how a succession of Glasnost/Perestroika strategies were orchestrated to keep communism alive under every Soviet leader since the U.S.S.R. was born on January 19, 1918. In each case the Glasnost/Perestroika strategy was a deception designed to fool the Western world into believing the Soviet Union was abandoning its communist ideology and was ready to join the community of nations. The code words used to mislead the American and West European public were terms such as "peaceful coexistence," "detente," "normalization" and "restructuring." The purpose of the Soviet deception was to disarm the West and obtain financial and technical assistance to continue increasing Soviet strength, pursuing their goals of global communism under their totalitarian rule.

The first make-believe reform was orchestrated by V. I. Lenin. His new communist paradise had so strangled industry and the economy that the U.S.S.R. was effectively bankrupt a short four years after its founding.

To obtain new life from the West, Lenin in 1921 renounced communism, fostered the image of moving toward a free enterprise economy and portrayed the reformed government as pro-Western. The deception was named the "New Economic Policy," or NEP. Gleeful western businessmen rushed in with millions in economic and technical assistance.

The party was short-lived. In less than five years the U.S.S.R. had consolidated its power, the Red Army was militarily armed and the people properly enslaved. The NEP was suddenly terminated, and the Iron Curtain came crashing down. The horrors enumerated in Professor Rummel's book were then systematically unleashed on the Russian people.

In the 1930s Stalin repeated the charade. The West again opened its arms, ignored all the evidence on the inherent evils of communism and the Soviet regime and sent massive aid that was again used to expand Soviet military capabilities and keep the population in chains.

Consider the threat against America made by a Soviet political strategist, Dimitri Manuilski, at the Lenin School of Political Warfare in the 1930s. It has never been retracted by any subsequent Soviet or Russian administration, including Yeltsin's. In fact both historical and contemporary events indicate that it has likely been central to their military and strategic policies which have placed America in perilous danger today. The Soviet/Russian overall strategy has been and continues to be "peace, peace; when there is no peace." Manuilski states:

> War to the hilt between communism and capitalism is inevitable. Today, of course, we are not strong enough to attack. Our time will come... To win, we shall need the element of surprise. The bourgeoisie will have to be put to sleep. So we shall begin by launching the most spectacular peace movement on record. There will be electrifying overtures and unheard of concessions. The capitalist countries, stupid and decadent, will rejoice to cooperate in their own destruction. They will leap at another chance to be friends. As soon as their guard is down, we will smash them with our clenched fist.[65]

Is there a specific Biblical warning about the potential for such sudden violence in an atmosphere of proclaimed peace?

For when they shall say, Peace and safety; then sudden destruction cometh upon them... (I Thes. 5:3).

Following World War II, Khrushchev repeated the deception which this time was called "peaceful coexistence." Its intent was anything but peaceful as the Soviet Union embarked on a massive effort to build a first-strike nuclear capability and increase its stranglehold over Eastern Europe. As it extended an olive branch to the West, it secretly redoubled its efforts to subvert free men and representative governments everywhere. In its plan of subversion, churches around the world were priority targets.

In 1967 Brezhnev introduced "detente" and used arms control as

> *In 1967 Brezhnev introduced "detente" and used arms control as the "carrot" to entice the West into curbing its military to show good faith.*

the "carrot" to entice the West into curbing its military to show good faith. Meanwhile, the U.S.S.R. unleashed another effort to surpass the West in military capability as a primary task in its expansion toward world domination. Again, Soviet military expansion was financed in large part on Western credit. Intelligence reports uncovered their plans, including their intended use of arms control to gain an advantage, but the West chose to ignore the information.

The United States, mindless of the realities of communism and Soviet practices, entered into good faith treaties with the U.S.S.R. such as ABM, SALT I & II, INF, and now START I & II. By 1980 the Soviet Union had achieved a first-strike capability and surpassed the United States in that arena by any nation's measure of effectiveness: missiles, warheads, throw weight, survivability, reliability and regular exercise of capabilities. Indeed it was this strength and the clear absence of a U.S. massive retaliation policy that led President Reagan to call for a new policy based on SDI which would defend America's cities and population.

Another Glasnost/Perestroika deception was launched in 1985 under Mikhail Gorbachev. As before, his objectives were to undermine U.S. military programs, specifically the SDI. He went all out to show how the Soviets were "Westernizing" in order to encourage the United States to support the "reasonable" Soviet leaders with economic and technical assistance. However, in typical Soviet fashion, while mouthing words of peace and restructuring to the West, he lectured his Soviet colleagues that they would never forsake their communist goals or stray from the path set by Lenin.

Soviet leader Mikhail Gorbachev proclaimed in a speech to the Politburo, November, 1987:

> Gentlemen, comrades, do not be concerned about all you hear about glasnost and perestroika and democracy in the coming years. These are primarily for outward consumption.... Our purpose is to disarm the Americans and let them fall asleep. We want to accomplish three things: One, we want the Americans to withdraw conventional forces from Europe. Two, we want them to withdraw nuclear forces from Europe. Three, we want the Americans to stop proceeding with Strategic Defense Initiative.[66]

In 1991 noted communist Politburo member Boris Yeltsin suddenly renounced communism and embraced "democracy" (Marx also called for democracy, depending upon how one defines it) and threw out Gorbachev in a bloodless coup. Our leaders instantly seized the high ground and claimed credit for the sudden victory in the Cold War. But the truth was quite different. Joseph D. Douglass, Ph.D., concluded, "In reality we never won the Cold War. The Soviets lost it, notwithstanding the efforts of the West, led by the United States, to keep them solvent, their totalitarian leaders in power and communism alive."[67]

Next we were told there was no remaining Soviet threat, nor could one be reestablished in less than a decade. While Soviet submarine missile forces and most of their land-based ICBMs remain intact and on station, none of the 3,500 strategic warheads are aimed at us, we were told.

That something was amiss should have been evident at least by September 14, 1993 when a *Washington Times* headline read, "Russian Nuclear Exercises Include Mock Hit On U.S." The lengthy article was based on interviews with top Clinton Administration military strategists and with Mr. Sven Kraemer, director of The White House Office of Arms Control for six years during the Reagan Administration. The Russians had reestablished effective control over all former Soviet strategic weapons

> *In reality, we never won the Cold War. The Soviets lost the Cold War notwithstanding the efforts of the West, led by the United States, to keep them solvent, their totalitarian leaders in power and communism alive.*

in the new Commonwealth of Independent States and were continuing with their strategic modernization programs. In unclassified testimony to Congress, the Defense Intelligence Agency reported that Russia then had in production 75 strategic ballistic missiles, eight strategic submarines and 20 bombers per year.[68] Moreover, these figures did not include the factories in the Ukraine that still produced ballistic missiles, bombers and ballistic missile defense components. In addition to production Russia's strategic modernization program included the development of two new land-based missiles (one a hard-to-find mobile system, of which the United States has none), a new submarine-based strategic missile, a new strategic ballistic missile submarine and construction of deep underground war-fighting bunkers. While proclaiming a need of economic support, Russia evidently had adequate resources to continue adding to its strategic nuclear arsenal.

The American strategists concluded that in view of the overwhelming evidence "...the Russian military still is making preparations to fight a nuclear war with the United States."[69] The Clinton Administration closed its eyes and ears and placed increased pressure on Congress to accelerate the U.S. unilateral disarmament. Dr. Douglass states:

> Through a variety of defectors we also learned that the Russians are no more complying with the chemical and biological warfare treaties than were their Soviet predecessors. We also learned that those capabilities are over ten times larger than intelligence had previously estimated and are potentially more powerful and extensive than their already formidable nuclear forces.[70]

Unquestionably, there have been massive changes in Russia, and more will come. But in what direction and to whose benefit is anyone's guess. The KGB is stronger than ever. The old communist bosses still rule, albeit with different titles, and have reconsolidated their base of power. Movements are under way to reestablish control over various "newly independent" states and breakaway republics.

Nevertheless, America, still sighing with relief over the end of the Cold War and the "death" of communism, continues to cut back its defenses. The course of the decline in American defense preparedness is shown in Figures 9 and 10.

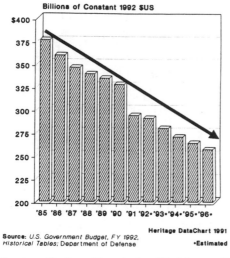

Observe the charts and
dates. Is America's
disarmament an acci-
dent or even a recent
"peacetime event"?

Courtesy Heritage Foundation, Washington, D.C.[71]

Figure 9. Defense Spending, 1985-1996

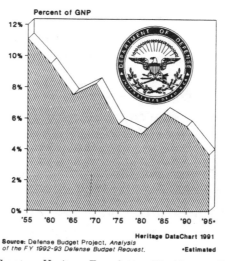

Courtesy Heritage Foundation, Washington, D.C.[72]

Figure 10. Defense Spending as a Share
of GNP

Figures 9 and 10 are based on government statistics. Their consequences were explained clearly in early 1991 in testimony given by then Secretary of Defense Dick Cheney and Joint Chief's Chairman General Colin Powell. Both men warned repeatedly that the drastic defense spending cuts would be dangerous to America's security unless there was a guarantee that the world would remain forever in a state of relative peace.[73] During one week in September of 1991, Sec'y. Cheney appeared on no fewer than five morning television shows to denounce U.S. efforts to "dismantle our own defenses."[74]

The Soviets' objectives have been largely achieved. Americans can ill-afford to place their hope in Russian leaders such as Boris Yeltsin, a lifetime hard-core Marxist/Leninist who rose to membership on the Politburo. As President of the Soviet Republic, he committed genocide against the freedom fighters, the people of the tiny province of Chechnya. "The army has conducted the war in Chechnya with terrible brutality. The Russians have leveled Grozny, the capital."[75] Can you imagine what it will be like for a disarmed United States under the UN-based New World Order, which is fast coming upon us?

The words of Manuilski and the pronouncements and actions of Gorbachev and Yeltsin should come as no surprise to anyone familiar with Marxism/Leninism and with Russian history since the Revolution. Far from being "dead," communism in Russia today is alive and determined to reconsolidate its power.

Peacekeeping But Not Peace

As we all know, peace is as elusive now as ever before. Yet the cutbacks in defense continue. Unimpeachable sources are now reporting that today the defense crisis has reached unprecedented, critical levels. The Army currently has only 50% of its 1990 Desert

Storm combat power. All four military services have run
short of money for training and for operations and maintenance. New weapons development has been cut to the
bone. To top it off, emphasis within the Department of
Defense has been deliberately refocused away from national defense to peacekeeping, humanitarian and other
"feel good" social services.

By official policy America has no ability to shoot
down even one incoming nuclear warhead, and plans to
defend America were torpedoed by our own Commander
in Chief.[76] In late 1995 President Clinton vetoed the
defense appropriations bill specifically to block the deployment of strategic missile defenses, SDI.

Today our cities have absolutely no ability to defend
themselves against a future Russian attack and are
equally vulnerable to attacks by a wide variety of countries like North Korea and Iran, both of which are
reported to be on
the edge of hav-
ing nuclear weap-
ons. Additionally,
according to au-
thorities, "At least
ten countries are

> *Especially worrisome, Communist
> China has been applying its new
> economic gains to further increase
> its military capability.*

expected to join them in the next couple years, and a
dozen will have developed biological and chemical weapons in that time."[77]

Especially worrisome, Communist China has been
applying its new economic gains to further increase its
military capability. In 1995 China launched a new offen-
sive directed against Taiwan. Their military presence
increased, and in January, 1996 China actually threatened missile strikes against Taiwan. As reported in the
New York Times on January 24, 1996, former Ambassador to China Charles Freeman was informed by a Chi-
nese official that China was prepared to act militarily
against Taiwan because "American leaders care more

about Los Angeles than they do about Taiwan." Mr. Freeman went on to specifically characterize this as "an indirect threat by China to use nuclear weapons against the United States." He might have added, 'and besides, the Americans have no missile defenses.'

These are only a few examples of what has been happening to us as the American people dream on about "peace." Since the early 1920s America, whose liberties were founded upon the Bible, the Ten Commandments, the preachings of Jesus Christ and an inerrant belief in God, has entered into good-faith military, economic and social exchange treaties with the atheistic U.S.S.R. This same government had committed genocide on its own citizens, had drenched in blood the countries added to its empire, a government which from its inception was sworn to the denial of God and annihilation of religion and freedom.

> *Nations such as North Korea, Libya, Iran, Iraq and Red China may soon be in a position to fire intercontinental missiles at America, delivering their nuclear warheads on our cities and our military installations.*

Over the years numerous Christian and conservative organizations and pro-defense movements such as the American Security Council did everything possible to sound the alarm to the American people as they watched stage after stage of unilateral dismemberment of our vital military defenses.

Nations such as North Korea, Libya, Iran, Iraq and Red China may soon be in a position to fire intercontinental missiles at America, delivering their nuclear warheads on our cities and our military installations. It seems basic that America should not disarm in the face of such increasingly formidable enemies and should at least go all out to build the best possible anti-missile defense system.

The UN international "peacekeeping" forces are now being expanded and strengthened in state-of-the-art weaponry. More importantly, these forces are being aided by the Clinton Administration.

Meanwhile, the American people continue their celebration of "peace," still rejoicing over the collapse of communism and the end of the Cold War. Chances are the Paul Reveres who continue to sound the alarm will be increasingly labeled by the media as "extremists," "paranoid" or an equivalent. All too many citizens, having lost their ability for Spiritual discernment, will blindly repeat the charges and ignore them or tolerate their tromping by the media.

If the American people were to surrender our nation's freedoms and sovereignty to a world government (there may be no choice if disarmament continues), which would impose its invincible military international police forces upon us, it would require little speculation to anticipate the fate of the Americans who believe in and support the continued independence and sovereignty of our God-given Judeo-Christian Republic.

The Power of Truth

It has always been the objective of tyrants to maximize Biblical ignorance of the masses of people because a Biblically literate populace is their most fearsome enemy. It has been said that wherever Jesus Christ has gone with His Gospel of salvation and His light of truth and Spiritual liberty, in His wake a great movement for political liberty has inevitably followed. *Ye shall know the truth, and the truth shall make you free* (John 8:32).

To illustrate, Hitler first outlawed God in the schools, then reduced the clergy to impotency, casting the most courageous ones into his death camps. Also, communist nations imposed the death penalty on civilians caught with a Bible or a Bible tract. Many American organizations smuggled Bible tracts into captive nations. Some were even delivered by helium-filled balloons driven by the winds. How could this have any effect at all on an evil government? The workers of darkness and iniquity understand the transforming power of even one page from God's Word. They also understand the threat posed by those who believe in that Word and would like nothing more than to eliminate Christians from the picture.

Human Nature and God's Purpose for National Independence

Whatever label a government chooses for itself, whatever respectable flag it chooses to drape around itself, this hard reality cannot be denied: given enough power, fallen man tends to enslave his fellow man, not liberate him. Founding Father John Adams, in expressing the overwhelming consensus of the Fathers, wrote that there has never been an example to the contrary in history. Adams entertained no illusions:

> In the institution of government, it must be remembered that, although reason ought always to govern individuals, it certainly never did since the Fall, and never will, till the Millennium; and human nature must be taken as it is, as it has been, and will be.[78]

Adams minced no words where human nature was concerned:

> There is no reason to believe the one much honester or wiser than the other; they are all of the same clay; their minds and bodies are alike.

> As to usurping others' rights, they are [all]
> equally guilty when unlimited in power.... [The]
> people, when they have been unchecked, have
> been as unjust, tyrannical, brutal, barbarous,
> and cruel, as any king or senate possessed of
> uncontrolled power. The majority has eternally,
> and without one exception, usurped the rights of
> the minority.[79]

The only thing that has prevented many of the nations from dropping their cloaks of respectability has been a general competition among them for commerce and aid from nations such as the United States. Many nations spend billions of dollars on propaganda for the purpose of respectability among other nations.

Under the New World Order in which national boundaries and sovereignty will have been swallowed up in a world government and a world military force, there will be no need for cosmetic restrictions on barbarity in any form. Thus, when God ordained as part of His plan for freedom that nations should have independent boundaries, His ordinance was in fact a form of a "restraining order" imposing a check on man's unbridled fallen human nature. (See Rom. 13:1-7, I Pet. 2:13-14.)

The Warnings from America's Patriots

Why have so many of America's Christians been deaf to the warnings of our nation's patriots? What strange force has such a grip over their minds as to render them blind, preferring to live in a non-controversial world of pretended "peace... when there is no peace?" Who's at fault? It all started in America's pulpits.

This ignoring of our military defenses is one of the deadliest and most glaring consequences of Abandonment Theology. The undiscerning vulnerability of the

American mind has resulted from the deranging of the vigilant dimension of the Christian faith in the ways earlier described. America's Christians today are in desperate need of Spiritual discernment and vision. The Abandonment Theologists have convinced them (including former President George Bush) that the United Nations New World Order is the way to peace.

Faith in man's essential "goodness" (in sharp contrast to his Biblically declared fallen human nature) is central to Marxist beliefs. A Marxist, who, like Hitler, is first and foremost anti-God, must believe that man is ultimately perfectible

> *If Marxists were to control the United Nations, and the United States were to surrender its sovereignty to the UN, who would stop the Marxists from achieving their grand aspirations for mankind by eliminating American Christians?*

and can thus achieve a social Utopia. The ultimate Utopia for the Marxist requires a purging of all who stand in their way. If the United States were to surrender its sovereignty to the UN, who would stop the Marxists from achieving their grand aspirations for mankind, beginning with the elimination of American Christians? Both Red China and Russia occupy permanent seats on the UN Security Council.

One great obstacle stands in the way of the final triumph of this global evil: the Christians of America. In all of history God alone has been able to turn back the advances of evil. No "religion" has been capable of freeing man and exalting the worth and dignity of the individual as has Christianity. (See Appendix A.)

There is only one answer. The hearts of the American people must be Spiritually reborn and the Word of God diligently searched by every able citizen, issue by issue, for His direction. Then and only then will America be able to save her torch of liberty from being extinguished and the world from plunging with her into the darkness that awaits all of us. There can be no substitute for an urgent nationwide revival of the faith.

America's Christians have a choice. We can allow our country and our freedoms to descend into oblivion by default, or we can choose to reject the deceptions of Satan and get back to the battlefronts as God commands us to do. The Fathers warned us that even the best Constitution cannot withstand the assault of tyranny if the hearts of the people have lost their Biblical morality and virtue.

Freedom (being Spiritual in its origin) begins in and flows out of the heart. The question, therefore, is not *"Can America sink into a global tyranny?"* The question is *"Will* her Christians let it happen?"

CHAPTER FOUR

DISARMING OUR MILITARY FROM WITHIN

Another Kind of Disarmament

America's Armed Forces are simultaneously under three forms of attack. Chapter Three was devoted to exposing the facts about the unilateral disarmament of our military weapons and defense systems. But there is another kind of disarmament that is afflicting our military fighting forces - the disarmament of their spirit, leading to a low morale and lack of "cohesion" through: (1) legalizing the admission of homosexuals into the Armed Forces; and (2) allowing women to serve in combat.

The triumph of the enemies of America in any one of the three areas of assault, two of those being termed by God as "abomination" (the antithesis of righteousness), may well prove fatal to our national security and our freedoms. If we allow our enemies to triumph in all three areas, we will surely bring God's judgment and destruction upon our nation. That is His promise to us: *All nations that forget God shall be turned into hell* (Psalm 9:17).

Homosexuals in the Military

America is dealing today with the homosexual issue as if God doesn't exist. Consider this overview of the

83

issues and our response to the assaults of the homosexuals, now a major political force.

For years homosexual organizations have attempted to convince the American people that homosexuality is simply another "lifestyle," that it is "genetic" and therefore is from God and that under the Constitution those citizens who practice it are entitled to "minority" civil rights protection. They claim that those who consider homosexuality to be a sin dangerous to society are guilty of "discrimination." The primary objective of the homosexuals has been to remove their foremost obstacle - the long-standing sodomy laws of the states and the military. Constitutional attorney John Eidsmoe writes:

> Sodomy was a criminal offense at common law and was forbidden by the laws of the original thirteen states when they ratified the Bill of Rights. ...Until 1961, all 50 states outlawed sodomy.[80]

In fact, nearly all nations of the world, for their own protection, have sodomy laws. The very term "crime against nature" is often used in law to define the prohibited act of sodomy.

Please note in Eidsmoe's statement the pivotal year 1961, bearing in mind the charts and graphs of Chapter Two are referenced to that period (when God was outlawed in the public schools). At the same time, 1961, when President John F. Kennedy launched a plan to disarm America of her military weapons and surrender her sovereignty to the United Nations, America's sodomy laws came under attack in many states. Eidsmoe continues:

> [By] 1993 [only] 24 states and the District of Columbia continue to provide criminal penalties for sodomy performed in private and between consenting adults.[81]

A primary objective of the homosexuals in targeting the military services was the removal of the Uniform Code of Military Justice ban on sodomy. Their efforts were unsuccessful until 1992 when presidential candidate Bill Clinton made a campaign promise to weaken then eliminate those sodomy laws which would result in the admission of gay and lesbian soldiers into the military. This gave the needed boost and credibility to the homosexuals who united from literally hundreds of activist groups and poured millions of dollars into the Clinton campaign producing, arguably, his margin of victory.[82]

The military chiefs of all the Armed Services, including Chairman of the Joint Chiefs General Colin Powell, Secretary of Defense Dick Cheney and General Norman Schwarzkopf, aggressively spoke out against removing the sodomy laws governing the military. They described the destructive effects of homosexuals on a soldier's morale, on unit "cohesion" and fighting effectiveness.

The military chiefs of all the Armed Services aggressively spoke out against removing the sodomy laws governing the military.

Gradually, their positions were filled by successors. The pressures from the Clinton Administration increased and became relentless. Resistance began to break. Finally, a sodomy-law compromise dubbed, "Don't Ask! Don't Tell!" resulted. This was a way for a limited number of homosexuals to gain admission to the military while the assault continued for the abandonment of sodomy laws and the unrestricted admission of homosexuals to all units of the Armed Forces.

For public propaganda purposes homosexuals have been portrayed as timid, persecuted "closet" people, more to be pitied than taken seriously. And the gullible, unsuspecting public, again abandoned by their clergy, have bought it, reflecting no concern or understanding of what it has done and is doing to America and our Armed Forces.

The Military Viewpoint

Former Chairman of the Joint Chiefs of Staff, retired Admiral Thomas Moorer, went on record:

> In the first place, these people are involved in what I consider to be a filthy, disease-ridden practice.[83]

Strong words, certainly in conflict with the image the public is being sold. What does Admiral Moorer mean by "disease-ridden?" Perhaps this study will help:

> Homosexuals are eight times more likely to have hepatitis than normal adults, 14 times more likely to have syphilis, and 5,000 times more likely to have AIDS. According to a massive 1991 study by the Family Research Institute, the median age of death for a homosexual not having AIDS was only 42 years, with a mere nine percent living to old age. Of 106 lesbians studied, the median lifespan was only 45 years, with 26 living to old age...[84]

What are homosexuals really like? Are they typically timid and non-aggressive? How will they adapt to the military lifestyle under the sodomy compromise "Don't Ask, Don't Tell" regulations? It has been said that to the homosexual "the military is a paradise."

It is no secret that despite claims to the contrary, homosexuality has nothing to do with romantic love as between a man and a woman. Rather, homosexuals *burn in their lust one toward another* (Rom. 1:27).

> The predatory nature of homosexuals is well documented in their own mainstream publications where they discuss the universal dream of

"all" homosexuals to 'finally make it with a straight hunk.'[85]

Male homosexuals often boast of many sexual encounters in a single day. Studies have reported that homosexual men have a median of 1,160 lifetime sexual partners.[86]

Is it any wonder why our soldiers, often living in close quarters including showering, use of bathrooms, bunking, and many field activities, would find a forced association with homosexuals highly destabilizing and demoralizing? In the gore and horrors of combat where "unit cohesion" can spell the difference between life and death, such an association can prove fatal not only to individual soldiers but to the entire unit.

> First-hand accounts from Army commanders...
> make a compelling case for the incompatibility
> of military life with open homosexuality. They
> also give a bird's eye view of the breakdown in
> morale, order and cohesion that result when a
> serviceman's homosexuality becomes known to
> his peers.[87]

Combat veteran Colonel Ronald D. Ray, USMCR(Ret.)* writes of the effect of homosexuals on the morale of combat soldiers:

> Particularly in the case of AIDS, the effect of
> nondetection could be devastating with regard
> to morale and combat readiness, if not life and
> health. Soldiers bleed in training and on the
> battlefield and are required to donate blood on

*Colonel Ronald D. Ray, USMCR(Ret.) author of *Military Necessity & Homosexuality*, historian, former Deputy Assistant Secretary of Defense (Reagan Administration), adjunct professor of law, Marine Reserve Judge-Advocate (1973-1984), decorated Vietnam combat veteran. Business address: 3317 Halls Hill Road, Crestwood, KY 40014

the battlefield at any given moment. As AIDS has a latency of three to six months (some evidence suggests years) before it can be detected by current testing methods, the possibility that it could be carried in a soldier's blood and either unwittingly or willfully be transmitted to another is greatly heightened if the military has no way of determining whether that soldier has had AIDS-efficient sex, the defining behavior of homosexuals. The homosexual movement also is demanding an end to HIV and AIDS testing as "discriminatory." [88]

Homosexuality and Genetics

Homosexuals have long contended that homosexuality is not learned but, rather, is genetic. Some theologians counter that such a claim is illogical because God would not give certain people a genetic code which produces characteristics that He calls "abomination" and thus curses.

There is now much research evidence which refutes the homosexual and supports the theologian. Let's consider the statement of Harold M. Voth, M.D., psychiatrist and psychoanalyst, Rear Admiral Medical Corps, USNR (Ret.):

There is no evidence whatsoever to support the gay community's claim that homosexuality is normal, freely chosen or caused by biological (genetic) factors. Theirs is nothing but a political (social) movement buttressed by untruths and misrepresented research and clinical studies: the goal is to perpetrate a gigantic hoax on society...[89]

Other scientific evidence comes from Judith A. Reisman, Ph.D.,* In response to this author's request for information she wrote:

> The theory of genetic homosexuality has been tried for decades, discarded even by biologist Alfred Kinsey, grandfather of the homosexual movement. The search for a "gay gene" is rendered critical today, as the public sees open homosexual recruitment in the schoolroom concomitant with a radical increase in males sexually abusing young boys — many of whom eventually die of AIDS. If early sexual abuse and poor fathering are keys to homosexuality, as they are keys to a myriad of other emotional disorders, then laws and conduct must change to protect the children, and that is a major threat to the homosexual lobby. Homosexual offenders would be punished and recruitment outlawed. Based on the most current viable, genetic research, homosexuality is largely nurture (learned) and not nature, which is why homosexuality always increases with increases in family dysfunction.[90]

Homosexuals do not procreate. Thus their "lifestyle" is actually a deathstyle. Civilization, if it depended upon homosexuals for its survival, would long ago have become extinct.

---

*Judith A. Reisman, Ph.D., scientist, listed in "Who's Who in Science & Engineering," research professor, author of numerous books including her classic *Kinsey, Sex and Fraud*. Institute for Media Education, Box 7404, Arlington, VA 22207

What God Says About Homosexuality

The ultimate answer as to who is right and who is wrong in every issue of life comes down to one thing: What does God the Creator and Giver of life and of all "natural" laws and processes have to say? He is the ultimate authority in all matters and through the Founding Fathers gave us America.

In the tradition of America's heritage let us turn to God for guidance and wisdom regarding homosexuality. Is homosexuality "of God"...just another "lifestyle" deserving of their claimed civil rights and minority status under the protection of our U.S. Constitution? God is explicit in what He thinks about homosexuality:

Thou shalt not lie with mankind, as with womankind: it is abomination (Lev. 18:22)

The New Testament carries the same message:

Wherefore God also gave them up to uncleanness through the lusts of their own hearts, to dishonor their own bodies between themselves:... For this cause God gave them up unto vile affections: for even their women did change the natural use into that which is against nature: And likewise also the men, leaving the natural use of the woman, burned in their lust one toward another; men with men working that which is unseemly, and receiving in themselves that recompense [payment] of their error which was meet [deserved] (Rom. 1:24,26,27).

---

* Other Bible references on homosexuality from both Testaments: Lev. 20:13; I Cor. 6:9,11; I Tim. 1:8 to 11; Jude 1:6,7.

There are numerous other references throughout the Old and New Testaments regarding homosexuality, always in the context of abomination to God.

In order that nobody in future generations could mistake His revulsion of homosexuality, God burned two cities, Sodom and Gomorrah, to ashes (see Genesis 19:24).

Homosexuals argue that the word "homosexuality" is not to be found in the Bible. Bible scholars claim that God articulated His position so clearly that nobody could misunderstand what He meant. Homosexuals also claim that Jesus was silent on homosexuality and must therefore have been in favor of it or at least had no objection to it. Was Jesus silent? He said: *Think not that I am come to destroy the law...: I am not come to destroy, but to fulfil* (Mat. 5:17). The law of Moses, given by God, calls homosexuality an abomination.

Governed by God or Ruled by Tyrants?

Well-meaning Christians throughout America are standing idle not because they lack love for our country or for our freedoms, or do not care about the people in our Armed Forces. They simply have no knowledge, because their would-be "watchmen-on-the-wall" clergymen are contentedly operating from their neutral, non-controversial, profitable reservations, refusing to become involved in a "political" issue - even in the middle of this holocaust to our faith, our nation and our youth. Does God think this is a "political" issue?

Can America continue on such a treacherous God-mocking path and survive the surrender of her Godly heritage? Will God let her survive? Has He let any such nation survive?

He answers the question:

All nations that forget God shall be turned into hell (Psalm 9:17)

Will the readers of this book take up the Call to Greatness and get into the battle where you are so desperately needed? William Penn bottom-lined the choice:

> Those who will not be governed by God will be ruled by tyrants.[91]

Women in Combat (Wives, Mothers, Daughters, Sisters)

Most people, even if they have never been on a battlefield, find objectionable the very thought of women being assigned to combat. This rejection becomes complete when they consider that the women who might be assigned to front-line combat could be their own wives, mothers, daughters and sisters. Why the spontaneous rejection? Because that's the way God made us. An awareness of our "natural" roles is born in us.

I asked one of America's most decorated combat veterans and military historians, Major General John K. Singlaub, U.S. Army (Ret.) what he thought about women being assigned to combat. He summed up his view in these words:

> This grotesque idea of deliberately placing our women into the most violent areas...of the most horrible violence the minds of men can create...is nothing less than an attack on our culture itself.[92]

In numerous interviews active and retired military combat veterans expressed views that are very much the same. Their sentiments range from proclaiming the idea is absurd to expressing outright anger. The problem is that many influential Washington politicians do not find the idea of women being assigned to hand-to-hand combat to be "grotesque" at all. In fact, the long established Department of Defense "Risk Rule," which has protected women in the military services from being placed too near the front line, has been eliminated.[93] Today women are on combat ships; they're flying combat warplanes; and soon they will be assigned to ground combat with men.

The next section examines what God says about men's and women's roles in life. Then what our government is saying is examined.

Created for Different Roles in Life

Although in our hearts and minds most of us know that putting women into combat is wrong, we also know that what God says is the determining factor which must guide our actions. God rejects homosexuality as an "abomination." He also rejects men and women exchanging roles. Read His own words:

> *The woman shall not wear that which pertaineth unto a man, neither shall a man put on a woman's garment: for all that do so are abomination unto the Lord thy God* (Deut. 22:5).

God is using a garment as an example to illustrate His general principle in nature. Again, as in the passages about homosexuality, He uses His term of revulsion, "abomination," to let us know the intensity of His position.

As set forth from Genesis throughout the Bible, God created male and female with defined purposes in life and with different mental, emotional and physical make-ups. They were designed purposefully for their respective roles.

God ordained man to be the protector and champion of his wife, his children, and his country. Combat is one of his duties. God designed a woman, however, to be a nurturer and care-giver. Combat is not one of her duties.

Other societal/business roles that women perform prove them to be equally as capable as men in carrying out most jobs, but that is no justification for allowing, or worse, deliberately putting women in harm's way in combat roles.

More to the point, if today a platoon of young women were fully as capable of hard combat ground fighting as a platoon of men, that platoon of women should not be allowed to fight in combat. Why? First and foremost, such an assignment would violate God's natural role for women, which is *not* to be in combat protecting men. Second, it would set a precedent which could open the way to conscription and involuntary combat assignment of other not-so-capable women.

What Proponents Say: A Matter of "Opportunity"? "Discrimination"?

Proponents of women in combat say it is a matter of "civil rights," that a woman as a citizen has just as much right to die in combat for her country as does a man, that she should be given that "opportunity" of "choice" and not be "discriminated" against because of her gender. Should America allow women (mothers, wives, sisters, daughters) to fight alongside men in ground combat? Senator Edward Kennedy (D. Mass.) and a host of other senators and congressmen say yes - that the criteria should not be gender, but "qualification."

On June 25, 1992 Senator Kennedy testified before the Presidential Commission on the Assignment of Women in the Armed Forces [PCAWAF]. He stressed that there should be no barriers or restrictions against women serving in combat and classified the existing statutes as "archaic." He proceeded to label them as "discrimination" and said that the real issue should be one of "qualification." Kennedy noted that Congress had repealed the statutes barring women from flying combat aircraft last year.[94]

Senator Kennedy has gone on record supporting women fighting alongside of men in combat. He also advocates involuntary assignment of women to infantry combat roles on a quota basis and proposed that women, up to now exempted from the draft, be subject to it equally with men.[95] When asked if the American people - the parents, husbands and families of their combat-bound women - had been consulted, Kennedy demonstrated his not-so-subtle contempt for them by citing this example:

> ...a unanimous Supreme Court decision, the Supreme Court didn't put their finger to the wind to find out...what the popular opinion was going to be.[96]

War in the Pentagon and Congress

Traditionally, the matter of who serves in the military has not been an issue of "choice" or "rights" or "equal opportunity." It always has been a matter of Department of Defense determinations on how wars can be fought and won with maximum "cohesion" among the combatants, efficiency and effectiveness. Former Secretary of Defense Dick Cheney put it this way:

> It's important for us to remember that what we are asked to do here in the Department of Defense is to defend the nation. The only reason we exist is to be prepared to fight and win wars.

We are not a social welfare agency...it is not a
jobs program. We aren't there to run social
experiments...[97]

Retired Army General Norman Schwarzkopf, former
Commander of Operations Desert Shield and Desert
Storm, spoke for many Americans when he declared:

Decisions on what roles women play in war
must be based on military standards, not
women's rights.[98]

An "Executive Summary" conclusion in the Report to
the President, Presidential Commission on the Assignment of Women in the Armed Services dated November
15, 1992, states:

The case for assigning women to combat fails for
the very basic reason that it is grounded princi-
pally in the concept of equal opportunity. When
national security is at stake, however, the need
to maintain a strong military must take prece-
dence over concerns about equal opportunity.[99]

Presidential Commissioner Charles Moskos testified in the "Summary":

...mixed-gender units, particularly as [they] get
closer to the combat area, have lower deployment rates, higher attrition, less physical
strength, more sexual activity, higher costs, et
cetera, et cetera.[100]

A war in the Pentagon and Congress over this issue
has been raging for a number of years. Various experiments placed women on war ships, and the results have
been consistently the same: a marked reduction in fighting efficiency.

In March, 1995 the Center for Military Readiness [CMR] Policy Analysis report cited in an article, "Pregnancy On The [aircraft carrier] U.S.S. Eisenhower:"

> Women have left the Eisenhower for medical reasons at a rate more than three times greater than men, primarily due to pregnancy. ...the ratio is approaching that recorded during Desert Shield and Storm, when pregnancies averaged about 10 percent, and women were 3 to 4 times as non-deployable as men...[101]

When considering the impact of women on combat readiness, Chief of Naval Operations Admiral Frank B. Kelso stated:

> We are, I think, at the ragged edge on readiness.[102]

The defense charts and graphs given in Chapter Three demonstrated that the unilateral disarmament of our nation's weapons systems has been no accident. Rather, it has direction, purpose (subordinating America's sovereignty to the United Nations) and time-lines. What we are witnessing today in the relentless political pressures for the introduction of women in combat roles is a step-by-step capitulation by the defense establishment over the protests of many of their most seasoned officers, active and retired, thus the courting of military disaster through reduced overall fighting efficiency.

The Department of Defense and Congress do not have to speculate about the results of allowing women in combat. There are historical precedents as to the destructive effects on those nations that have done this, including Israel and Russia. These countries met with disaster "at the front" and had to withdraw their women.

At Stalingrad the Russian soldiers would leave
their posts to find and protect their women.[103]

The godless drive to "gender-norm" women with men
in combat roles has resulted in the creation of a double-
standard - one for men, a compromised one for women.
For example:

> ...an extraordinary pattern of special privileges
> and "flexible" standards [was] permitted for two
> female F-14 pilots, one of whom was Navy Lt.
> Kara Hultgreen, who was killed...while attempt-
> ing to land on the carrier U.S.S. Abraham Lin-
> coln... .Specific records obtained by CMR [Cen-
> ter for Military Readiness]* and compiled in our
> Special Report on Double Standards in Naval
> Aviation indicate that F-14 instructors gave Lt.
> Hultgreen low scores and four... unsatisfactory
> performance "downs" in training - one or two of
> which are frequently sufficient to end an avia-
> tion career.[104]

In America allowing women to fight in combat in any
of the Armed Forces, whether they want to or not, flies in
the face of our Christian culture and heritage. God will
not tolerate it any more than He will tolerate our breaking the sodomy laws. If we want to stay free, we must live
by God's rules, not our own.

*Center for Military Readiness, P.O. Box 2324, Livonia, MI 48151: Elaine
Donnelly, president & former member of the Presidential Commission on
the Assignment of Women in the Armed Forces (PCAWAF) by appointment
of President George Bush

Women in the Military - Ground Combat Speculation

The foregoing discussion is not to challenge the correctness of women serving in non-combatant roles as they always have in the military. Such support roles are entirely in harmony with God and our defense of America's God-given freedoms.

Let's assume for this discussion that the current corrosive trend toward granting women ground combat roles is accomplished. What could it be like for them on the battlefield? Of course, there are limitless scenarios so let's consider just one.

In the Persian Gulf War 40,000 women were called to serve. Some mothers still nursing infants were separated from them. Her service behind the lines could well have become the equivalent of front-line service had victory been less sudden.

Strange things happened which preempted much bloodshed. For example, a strong desert wind suddenly blew the sand off thousands of Iraqi land mines which would have killed great numbers of our soldiers. Tens of thousands of body bags were on hand but went unused. Great numbers of women soldiers, had they been committed to ground combat roles, could have died together with male soldiers trying to save the women or help them. More wars are inevitable, but their outcomes may not be as happy as the Persian Gulf War. General Schwartzkopf was a brilliant strategist, but he had, on multiple occasions, considerable unpredictable assistance from Nature. Even so, five women died in that war.

When gender-norming is considered, the vast majority of women do not have the stamina for the rigors of combat. In fact,

> ...women on average have about 40-50% less upper body strength, and 20-30% less stamina

and endurance, both of which are crucial for survival and effectiveness in combat units.[105]

Our women may suddenly find themselves in hand-to-hand combat with men of far superior strength and agility. The weapons in this type of battle include knives, bayonets, wires for strangling and an endless assortment of up-close devices designed to mutilate and kill. We would be subjecting our women to total violence.

Man's natural tendency is to be the protector of women, and when confronted with conditions in which women are threatened his natural chivalry will likely direct his behavior. The historical fact is that since the beginning of civilization men have fought and died to protect their women. Why? Because they were born that way.

This is what other nations have found when they committed their women to combat. Orders were disobeyed, discipline was destroyed, unit "cohesion" was ruined and the all-important "morale and spirit" so essential to victory were lost.

For the proponents of women in combat who set forth a seemingly righteous argument that "No woman should be denied the opportunity to serve in any military position...," the obvious retort is that permitting our nation's women to get slaughtered on the battlefield is not classifiable as an "opportunity." Rather, it is symbolic of an advanced state of moral and cultural decadence of a nation abandoning the centerpiece of its greatness - the family institution.

Where Are the Clergy?

What possible explanation can there be as to why the clergy and Christian men of America remain silent and tolerate such unspeakable and barbaric proposals for

their women, unless they have lost all Spiritual awareness of their God-mandated duties as men and guardians
of their loved ones?

> *His watchmen are blind: they are all ignorant,*
> *they are all dumb dogs, they cannot bark; sleep-*
> *ing, lying down, loving to slumber* (Isa. 56:10).

A Final Warning

In 1993 Colonel Ronald Ray, attorney, decorated
combat veteran, former Deputy Assistant Secretary of
Defense, was interviewed by Dr. James Dobson on his
nationwide radio broadcast, "Focus On The Family," on
the topic "women in combat" and "homosexuals in the
military." Col. Ray, having served in the Pentagon, knew
personally a great many of the top military leaders
including the Joint Chiefs. He said on the program:

> Your listeners need to know that naked political
> pressures have been brought to bear to a degree
> that I have never seen in my 32 years experience
> in the military or in the Pentagon. The service
> chiefs have been subjected to intimidation and
> pressure and they appear to be ready to
> accommodate...women in combat which is
> against their best military judgment, ...The
> courts, under the doctrine of Military Necessity,
> have deferred to the best military judgment of
> our senior military leadership, but their best
> military judgment is being perverted, distorted,
> and turned on its head.

> The most compelling testimony I heard last year
> was from David Horowitz, a former radical
> whose mother and father were both commu-

nists, and who said, "I was dedicated to the subversion and overturning of every American institution," and he said, "Ladies and gentlemen of the Commission, we were successful in subverting and overturning every American institution but one - it was the military institution." He said, "Why don't you wake up? Women in combat and homosexuals in the military is to finish the job on the only institution that survived the 60s and 70s revolution intact,..."

CHAPTER FIVE

THE NATURE OF THE STRUGGLE

For we wrestle not against flesh and blood,
but against principalities, against powers,
against the rulers of the darkness of this world,
against spiritual wickedness in high places.
Ephesians 6:12

A Clash of Worldviews

The real battlegrounds in America's struggles are the minds and hearts of her people. Most battlefield wars, including acts of genocide and "ethnic cleansing," are culminations of clashes over conflicting ideas, acute differences in worldviews.

"The fundamental question of ethics is who makes the rules? God or men? The theistic answer is that God makes them. The humanistic answer is that men make them. This distinction between theism and humanism is the fundamental division in moral theory."[106]

Dr. Tim LaHaye, in his book *The Battle for the Mind,* expressed it, "In this world there are two basic lines of reasoning that determine the morals, values, life-styles and activities of mankind - the wisdom of man or the wisdom of God."[107] (See I Cor.1:17-25.)

Regarding man's wisdom, in all of recorded history neither secular humanism with its pantheistic religions nor atheistic Marxism/Leninism has produced anything but tyranny, misery and enslavement. This is understandable because, as God sets forth in Jeremiah 17:9,

The heart is deceitful above all things, and desperately wicked. This is referring to the heart of "fallen" unregenerate man.

The secular humanist looks to himself and his finite vision, not to God, as the source of truth and final authority. His "situational ethics" recognize no absolute standards of morality and truth. The "wisdom of man" is therefore no true wisdom at all because its maximum depth of perception can only be based upon life's finite experiences and observations.

There is a way that seems right to a man, But its end is the way of death (Prov. 14:12). With no eternal value system or standards for truth the secular humanist is an easy victim of Satan, the master of deceit, and is highly vulnerable to enlistment into his cause.

In total contrast *Where the Spirit of the Lord is, there is liberty* (II Cor. 3:17). The absolute, unchanging Word and truth of God spans the generations: *...his truth endureth to all generations* (Ps. 100:5). Thus, the underlying nature of America's struggles is truly spiritual as Satan manifests himself through godless men, while Christ manifests Himself through true believers.

> *For we wrestle not against flesh and blood, but against principalities, against powers, against the rulers of the darkness of this world, against spiritual wickedness in high places* (Eph. 6:12).

Distilling the above relentless, spiritual warfare into the issues - the practical nature of the struggles afflicting and destroying our country - the question arises, is there a solution? Is there a victorious way out of the multitude of crises afflicting our country?

It seems that in recent years just about everything has been getting progressively worse, from family relationships to government policies to wars around the world. Let's consider how we got into this alarming situation.

For several decades after the 1962 Supreme Court decision America continued to turn her back on God and underwent a gradual moral deterioration and loss of purpose and greatness that today have rendered her weak where she should be strong, corrupted when she should be virtuous and accelerating toward collapse into a godless, humanistic world government that will enslave her children.

Figure 1, below, as shown on page 3, represents America under siege with the battleground being spiritual, political, ideological, economic and military. What does the total picture look like?

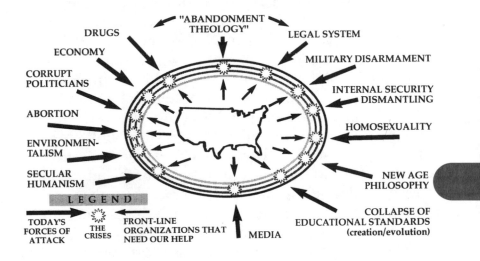

(1) Whereas most people have an idea about some of the spheres of the attacks against America's liberties and foundations of freedom, they have no concept of the total picture wherein the assaults appear to be coordinated and simultaneous.

Studying Figure 1 leads to only one conclusion: what is happening and has been happening for several decades is no accident.

(2) The assaults are not without resistance. In fact our country has no shortage of "Paul Reveres." We don't have to look into the pages of history to find the great heroes and patriots of our nation. We have but to open our eyes - they're all around us. Though long engaged in slow, painful retreat, these dauntless men and women have actually bought us the time that may make the difference between whether America perishes in the tidal wave of evil that is engulfing her or makes a comeback to greatness.

"Greatness" results when a nation draws near to God and obeys Him: *Draw nigh to God, and he will draw nigh to you* (James 4:8); *Fear God, and keep his commandments: for this is the whole duty of man* (Eccl. 12:13).

(3) There is a "positive" way to read Figure 1. It is a picture of the Biblical or Christian Worldview in many of its dimensions. Few people realize that God, the Author of our liberties, speaks through the Bible to every one of those topics, defines the enemies of freedom and sets the believer's course for victory. There is no reason for America's Christians to be confused about the multitude crises afflicting our country or how to triumph over all of them, except from lack of diligence in reading and applying the Scriptural solutions (See Ps. 1).

Confusion, loss of vision and loss of greatness result when the total picture is fragmented and the issues stand alone. Professor Ron Nash states it succinctly:

Christianity...is a complex, large-scale system of belief which must be seen as a whole before it is assessed. To break it up into disconnected parts is to mutilate and distort its true character. We can, of course, distinguish certain elements in the Christian faith, but we must stand back and see it as a complex interaction of these elements. We need to see it as a metaphysical system, as a worldview, that is total in its scope and range.[108]

The triumph of the Abandonment Theologists and the secular humanist enemies of America's freedoms has been to destroy the Christian's perception of the total faith as an all-encompassing metaphysical system, a worldview. They do this by breaking it up into disconnected parts, mutilating and distorting its true character. Thus they have succeeded in wrecking the ability of Christians to envision their role in the total Biblical Worldview, to rightly divide truth from error and to take the necessary actions in the defense of their God-given freedoms.

For example, the probable reason why the Book of Genesis is the most attacked book in the Bible is that it offers a total life view for individuals. It explains God's purpose for independent nations and why He is outspokenly opposed to world government which is the enemy of individual freedoms. Genesis tells us where we came from, that we are special creations made in the image of God (not products of dog-eat-dog evolution), why we are here, what is our mission and what are our duties. It establishes the family institution.

Genesis assures us of our accountability to God at a future judgment which holds rewards and punishments. It deals in a trinity - the past, the present and the future - and gives meaning, purpose, direction and fulfillment to life in all of its realms. Without the total picture life can indeed be dreary, devoid of purpose and self-destructing. Without purpose and the high calling of God, the people are easily enslaved. Such is increasingly America's condition today as she abandons her obedience to Him.

It has been said that the most horrible, destructive sin that can be committed against the youth (the sacred trust and future) of a free nation is to rob them of their sense of Divine calling and purpose by convincing them that they are not born in the image of God. Such is and has been the root of the damage rendered for several decades against the youth of America as the Abandonment Clergy and millions of professing Christians stood on the sidelines.

> *Contrary to all governments founded upon atheistic secular humanism or Marxism/Leninism, the Christian Worldview establishes the value of the individual as being infinite in the eyes of God.*

The Biblical Worldview addresses every aspect of a person's and a nation's life. It is the very spirit and essence of the Declaration of Independence, the separation of powers structure of our government and the civil laws of the Constitution and Bill of Rights.

Contrary to all governments founded upon atheistic secular humanism or Marxism/Leninism, the Christian Worldview establishes the value of the individual as being infinite in the eyes of God, that every person is born "in the image of God" and has certain "unalienable rights among which are life, liberty and the pursuit of happiness." That does not mean that each person is necessarily born politically free but rather has a God-given right to freedom. No man can take away that right to freedom because it is from God. Man does have a Divine right to fight for freedom, and if he inherited it, as we did from the Founding Fathers, he has the duty and responsibility to fight for it not only for his own generation but to preserve it for posterity.

The political government is established to protect those rights, and the government is therefore the servant of the people, whose handbook for monitoring and directing the actions of their political representatives is the Bible. Accordingly, the Bible, whose principles of liberty and moral codes are eternal and unchanging, was the foundational book in all public education when our country was established.

At the same time, the Bible is the greatest political book ever written. In exchange for the liberties available through it, God assigns to the individual many responsibilities and duties. There was never, and is not today, a First Amendment "two-way wall of separation" between church and state. Such a "wall" would have to be contrived because it flies in the face of His mandates. Duties and responsibilities of the citizens are imperative for the maintenance of their God-given liberties.

It bears repeating that all of the Founding Fathers, including supposed deists Franklin and Jefferson, were scholars of the Bible and were outspoken advocates of the Christian Worldview. That was the bonding agent which bridged denominations and gave birth to our American Constitutional Republic. No law was ratified that was not rooted in the Bible.

After the founding of America, whose Constitution and freedoms became the light and inspiration for a wretched, mostly enslaved world, our country's greatness - that is, the greatness of her people - was recognized by the world. She became unmatched in commerce, generosity, all manner of virtues and military might.

From time to time when Biblical morality became compromised and corresponding corruption set in, great Spiritual revivals swept the land, and the Christian Worldview Biblical standard was restored, together with its countless blessings of Biblical vision, discernment, prosperity and military power. This same kind of Spiritual revival is desperately needed in America today.

The mission of Jesus Christ was that of freedom. In that cause He came, and in that cause He went to the cross. He taught the primacy of the spirit and the worth and dignity of the individual. In contrast the secular humanist and Marxist/Leninist teach that there is no spirit; therefore an individual has no inherent dignity or Divine right to freedom.

Christianity as a worldview holds a position on virtually every subject that pertains to life, its meaning and purpose. Its handbook, the Bible, is considered to be the Word of God and therefore infallible in all of its instructions.

> *Those who hold the atheistic worldview of secular humanism and the atheistic worldview of Marxism / Leninism are easy victims of Satan.*

America is in trouble today because her people have followed their Abandonment Clergy who have trivialized and watered down the Biblical Worldview messages of God on many crucial freedom issues. The consequent loss of Spiritual vision and discernment has made Americans easy victims for Satan's deceptions.

Those who hold the atheistic worldview of secular humanism or of Marxism/Leninism because they lack the wisdom of God and possess no Spiritual defenses are readily enlisted into Satan's service.

In abject contrast to America's independent, sovereign Constitutional Republic, both worldviews are wellsprings for socialism and/or communism and ultimately lead to world government.

The nature of America's struggles today, therefore, is the conflict between the worldviews of entrenched secular humanism, which can lead only to a loss of liberty, and its opposite, the Christian Worldview, upon which America was founded and which is the wellspring freedoms. It is a war of ideas that is being waged in many spheres including theological, ideological, political, economic and military. It is spiritual in its essence, and in every sphere it reduces down to the masters of deceit vs. the people of God. The outcome of the battles and America's future will be determined by whether or not America's Christians are willing to turn back to God in full submission and obedience before the bell finally tolls. The remnant Christians are exerting every possible effort to that end and are the principal obstacle to the triumph of world government over our nation.

The Teaching of Evolution

Let's consider another example of opposing worldviews which the American people have not understood and which require urgent corrective attention: the teaching of evolution in the schools as reality and fact.

Evolution - it sounds harmless. In fact, as a friend once commented to me, "I couldn't care less whether I got here as a result of two love-sick amoebas that washed up on a shore a zillion years ago and through a process of natural selection (dog-eat-dog survival of the fittest) resulted in me, or whether I am a special creation of God."

Let's consider a few of the implications of evolution, which has long been indoctrinated into our young ones in the public school system.

The first target of the evolutionists is an understanding of and appreciation for our American heritage passed to us from the Founding Fathers. If our heritage isn't appreciated and understood, it will be lost. One or two generations are all that is required.

The first victims would be our Declaration of Independence and our Constitution because the Declaration establishes God, not the secular state, as the Author and

Giver of all freedoms and human rights. It says we are created by God with certain "unalienable" rights including "life, liberty and the pursuit of happiness." The Constitution, whose civil laws are all rooted in the Bible, established the framework for liberty within which America's individual citizens may pursue happiness.

In a word, the American political system is founded upon the Biblical concept, that is, the Christian Worldview, of the primacy of the spirit, the worth and dignity of the individual, one nation under God in which the purpose of the political government is to safeguard the freedoms of the citizens (see Rom. 13:1-4). The Divine responsibility of the citizens is to elect God-fearing righteous men and women to office and hold them accountable so that their activities conform to Biblical standards.

Evolution denies a loving, personal, intervening freedom-giving God Who created man in His own image, sent His Son to show

> *God established freedom and national independence as inseparable. They are the seedbed of "life, liberty, and the pursuit of happiness."*

us the Way and to die in the cause of Spiritual and political freedom. Yet, godless evolution has been drummed into the minds of our young people for decades by the secular humanists through John Dewey's Progressive Education while God has been outlawed in the classrooms by the U.S. Supreme Court.

God's Position on National Independence and the New World Order

What is the God-ordained relationship between individual freedom, national government and national boundaries? What would God say about the New World Order, now termed the New Civilization, a world military force and one-world government? Dr. H. Edward Rowe summarizes the government's intent:

(1) The Sovereign God of the Universe, who created man, established nations and assigned their boundaries as the framework for the life of man on earth (See Gen. 10:31-32, Deut. 32:8) to provide an environment within which men might enjoy the freedom to "seek the Lord" and serve Him (See Acts 17:26-27, I Tim. 2:1-4).

(2) As the Founding Fathers noted, man exists in a fallen state of spiritual and moral depravity and is naturally selfish, cruel and aggressive toward his fellow man. God has ordained that national governments shall secure and perpetuate internal order and individual freedom.[109] (See Rom. 13:1-7, I Pet. 2:13-14).

Political freedom, being of God, is a Spiritual concept. In fact the very mission of Christ was that of freedom, both Spiritual and political. Political freedom frees man to serve God with all of his mind, heart and strength in every dimension of life and to enjoy boundless blessings given in return for such loyalty. Political freedom inevitably flows out of Spiritual freedom *from the bondage of corruption into the glorious liberty of the children of God* (Rom. 8:21).

God, the Author of freedom, established freedom and national independence as inseparable. They are the seedbed of "life, liberty and the pursuit of happiness." God gifted us with "volition," the right to choose the road we will take. *I set before you life and death, blessing and cursing: therefore choose life, that both you and your descendants may live* (Deut. 30:19). He wants us to choose life, but it's up to us. If we choose life, total commitment and obedience will be required.

How does God describe the relentless spiritual wars that are behind all temporal wars? What does He say about our responsibilities? How involved does He want us to be? Can there be "peace in our time"?

We cannot live our lives as independent, self-sufficient, self-serving individuals insulated from the influence of invisible forces. Many people deny the spiritual dimension altogether. They comment, "If I can't see it, I won't believe it." Can we "see" gravity? No. Does that mean it doesn't exist and is not ever-present? So it is with the invisible spiritual dimension of our life experiences. In the Bible we read about invisible, living, active spiritual realities as they affect our personal lives. Those spirits, representing God and Satan, light and darkness, are in relentless competition for the possession of and influence over our mortal minds. Their nature and objectives are opposites.

Light vs. Darkness

Jesus said, *I am the light of the world: he that followeth me shall not walk in darkness, but shall have the light of life* (John 8:12). Light is joy, happiness, success, prosperity, freedom to give and to receive in proportion. It is inner peace, freedom from the bondage of sin and corruption, political freedom, Spiritual vision, Spiritual discernment, Biblical knowledge and wisdom, the power to be victorious over our adversaries on both the spiritual and temporal planes, hope and the assurance of eternal life. Light is life (see III John 2).

What is truth? Light is truth. *I am the way, the truth, and the life* (John 14:6). God's law is truth (See Ps. 119:142); God's commandments are truth (See Ps. 119:151); God's Word is truth (See John 17:17); Christ is truth (See John 14:6).

Darkness is the opposite of Light. *The thief cometh not, but to steal, and to kill, and to destroy* (John 10:10). Darkness is confusion, of which Satan is the author (See I Cor. 14:33), resulting in lack of Spiritual vision and discernment, misery, suffering, political enslavement and death for us all. Satan is Darkness.

Satan has no other mission but to steal - steal the blessings of God such as life, liberty, prosperity and happiness - and to kill and destroy. He is the archenemy of Christ. He is the fallen element in fallen human nature. He is tyranny, slavery and death. He knows no mercy and never rests (See I Pet. 5:8). God describes those who have fallen captive to Satan: *Their feet are swift to shed blood: Destruction and misery are in their ways: And the way of peace have they not known: There is no fear of God before their eyes* (Rom. 3:15-18).

Christ's Battle Cry

The Son of God was manifested that he might destroy the works of the devil (I John 3:8).

Christ gave His mission statement in His first sermon in the temple: *[H]e hath anointed me to preach the gospel to the poor;... to preach deliverance to the captives, and recovering of sight to the blind, to set at liberty them that are oppressed* (Luke 4:18). Jesus will save you; Satan will destroy you. Christ liberates individuals and nations who obey Him. As long as they maintain their vigilance, Satan cannot prevail because through the Holy Spirit Christians have the supreme power. But God does allow Satan to exist, and when that nation, once free and showered with blessings, loses its vigilance, becomes "lukewarm" and turns away from God, after a certain point God will remove His protective hand and allow

Satan to drive that nation to destruction and enslavement. Such is the state that America is approaching today. No humanistic, strategic plans based on reason alone will save our country. Logic has no power in a spiritual war. We must first acquire that power by turning to God - to Christ, the Author of our freedoms.

CHAPTER SIX

ALL NATIONS THAT FORGET GOD...

All nations that forget God shall be turned into hell.
Psalm 9:17

The Retreat

What does it mean to "forget God"? The answer is vital to America's destiny. Is "remembering" a simple act of acknowledging that God is indeed Lord and reciting a list of His attributes as is often set forth in songs of praise?

Every Christian is called by God to the highest level of personal character and virtue, to a *knowledge* of the Source of his and her freedoms and of their duty to defend and perpetuate those freedoms. If that sense of loyalty and responsibility is destroyed - if the Ten Commandments are outlawed along with prayer and Bible reading in the schools and our youth deprived of knowledge of their heritage - then we cannot be far from Witherspoon's prediction that our Constitution will collapse - and with it, our liberties.

As previously discussed, much of the clergy, along with their millions of victimized American Christians following their pastors' lead, have retreated from the battlefront to the social, non-confrontational, non-controversial reservation. They say that Christians should confine their religious activities to politically non-controversial roles and keep their Bibles out of the political process. They also say that based on prophecy these are the "last days," and any efforts we make to restore righteousness to this nation will be in vain and need not even be undertaken.

Expressions such as the "New Age," the "post-Christian era" and the "New World Order" have come into vogue and are often heard and accepted in church services and Sunday School classes with little protest. We are assured, however, by the Abandonment Clergy that God is in control of all events and if we are "born again," we and our loved ones will be taken from this world in the "rapture." They say our job now is to love Christ, worship Him, adore Him, lead virtuous personal lives, keep Christ out of the political arena and be sure the two-way wall of separation between church and state remains high and impregnable. After all, politics is no business of the church.

The following story helps illustrate this point. I heard one of America's best-known theologians say the following on a nationwide broadcast:

> You know, folks, people call my office and ask, "Dr.__, don't you love your country? You're always so negative about it and unwilling to get into the battle." I respond, "Of course I love my country, and I love living here. I love my freedoms, but I have to face the fact that America is on the way down as was ancient pagan Rome, and she will meet the same horrible fate because of her sins. My concern is not for a country that is finished but rather for the kingdom of God. I love my family, and my concern is that they be right with God and concern themselves with the kingdom where nothing that happens on earth can affect their salvation and immortal souls."

The answer to that clergyman's position is that ancient pagan Rome was always pagan. In contrast America was created in Jesus Christ and the Bible. America was *never* pagan. God's mandate when the nation strays is for its faithful to *stand fast in the liberty wherewith Christ hath made us free* (Gal. 5:1) and to come forth and engage in the battle. In Psalm 94:16 He asks, *Who will rise up for me against the evildoers? or who will stand up for me against the workers of iniquity?*

Theologian Dr. R. C. Sproul charges such clergymen who disengage from this world with trading on "the narcotic effect of ecclesiastical opium." This is precisely the condition sought and hoped for by those who would conquer and enslave the American people, anticipating that with the teeth having been pulled from their faith they would surrender their heritage without a fight under the promise of pie in the sky and salvation without responsibility. Dr. Sproul wrote in *Classical Apologetics*:

> Other religions may choose a radical denial of this world, seeking asylum in a supratemporal sphere of mystical otherworldliness; but Christianity enjoys no such luxurious option. Attempts by Christians, past or present, to quit this world in ascetic retreat betray a tacit denial of the most elemental principles of the Christian view of creation and redemption.[110]

Clearly, the Christian's mandate in our crisis world is to stand and fight in the cause of God. Abandoning ship should be unthinkable to an American Christian knowledgeable of his or her heritage and duty to Christ and of the consequences of defeat. Yet the Abandonment position is common through much of the American church.

Would Christ agree with the philosophy of abandoning the ship of America that He created, a philosophy which has been taught by the clergy of the last few decades? Would He consider it glorifying to the Father?

Dr. Sproul comments on the church today:

> The church is safe from vicious persecution at the hands of the secularist.... So long as the church knows her place and remains quietly at peace on her modern reservation. Let the babes pray and sing and read their Bibles, continuing steadfast in their intellectual retardation; the church's extinction will come not by sword or pillory, but by the quiet death of irrelevance. It will pass away with a whimper not a bang.[111]

Dr. Sproul continues:

> But let the church step off the reservation, let her penetrate once more the culture of the day and the Janus-face of secularism will change from benign smile to savage snarl.[112]

The Other Side of Love

> *This is love, that we walk after his commandments* (II John 6).

Abandonment Theology's rallying banner is "love." Ask anyone on the abandonment reservation, "Do you love the Lord with all of your heart and with every ounce of passion that is in you?" The answer will come back as a thunderous *"Yes!"* "Do you love your country?" *"Yes!"* The fact is that they will mean it, and their hearts will be as devoted to the cause of Christ as any could be.

If we were to examine their bank accounts, we would find impressive examples of generosity to hospitals, orphanages, churches, educational institutions, all manner of benevolences and charities. Surely, God would be pleased. Undeniably, love is giving of one's resources and of one's self. Its virtues include compassion, tenderness, helping a brother and feeding the poor.

But that's only a part of the meaning of love. What's missing from their definition of love is the action dimension - the "war cry" of confrontation against evil. What happened to it? Certainly the Founding Fathers lived by the war cry, won against seemingly impossible odds and gave us our Constitutional Republic.

How is it that so many of America's Christians have ended up on neutral reservations? Have they intentionally defected from the battlefront? Have they knowingly abandoned their sacred Christian duty in our crisis world? Of course not! Then why the retreat?

> *The Abandonment Clergy have taken Christ's most commanding, demanding charge - love - and subtly removed its firepower, its major action dimension, and reduced it down to simply a sentiment of compassion.*

The Abandonment Clergy have taken Christ's most commanding, demanding charge - love - and subtly removed its firepower, its major action dimension, and reduced it down to simply a sentiment of compassion. What have the clergy extracted?

Love is expressed in numerous ways throughout the Scriptures, but it all comes down to one definition: Love is obedience to the commandments (See I John 5:3). But if God's commandments are truth (See Ps. 119:151), and God is truth (See John 14:6), then the commandments by definition represent a declaration of war against evil in all of its manifestations.

A born-again Christian is one who has committed his or her life to the service of Christ and thus pledges obedience to the commandments. The commandments represent a battle cry of righteousness and a war cry to engage the workers of iniquity on every front.

Christ proclaimed that He had come to *destroy the works of the devil* (I John 3:8). A born-again Christian, indwelt and empowered by the Holy Spirit in the cause of truth and liberty, belongs on the front lines of the action according to his calling (See II Pet. 1:10), not in the bleachers watching his God-given country crumble and not on the reservation socializing in the midst of the holocaust.

According to the Bible a Christian's commitment to action is not an option. Whatever his reasons for abandoning the battlefront in preference for the social reservation, even if he is a victim of the Abandonment Clergy, the consequences to his country and loved ones will be the same. How he will fare with God at the Judgment is another subject.

The Question of Works and Salvation

Are "works" really necessary to salvation? Can one lose his salvation by not doing good works? What does James mean when he says: *But wilt thou know, O vain man, that faith without works is dead?*(Jas. 2:20).

If we are saved by "grace," not by "works," why bother doing works? If works are not important, why did Jesus say, *I wish that you were hot or cold; but because you are lukewarm, I will spue you out of my mouth* (Rev. 3:15-16)? If "God is in control," are works necessary for the triumph of freedom over tyranny, righteousness over evil?

The Founding Fathers would have had no difficulty in answering these questions. But many Christians today do have difficulty because their Abandonment Clergy have sold them a doctrine of "salvation without responsibility," and their confusion is leading them and their children into darkness by default. *Where there is no vision, the people perish* (Prov. 29:18).

If America is finished and has passed the point of no return, as the Abandonment Clergy are preaching, do works really matter? Some contend that works are the same as legalism and that legalism - winning God's favor by your works - is precisely what Christianity rejects. This position looks to the Apostle Paul for its Scriptural support. Paul writes,

> *For by grace are ye saved through faith; and that not of yourselves: it is the gift of God: Not of works, lest any man should boast* (Eph. 2:8-9).

On the surface this great truth would seem to negate the value of works in God's eyes or would at least relegate works to a secondary position having nothing to do with one's personal salvation and heavenly destination. The argument says this: we live in a fallen, lost world which ultimately is destined to perish, together with our works. What truly counts, then, is our personal salvation and that of our loved ones because salvation is eternal while the world - and works - are transient.

If that were the sum total of the Christian salvation experience, then perhaps works really are not that important to God. But this reference to works speaks specifically to the issue of salvation. Paul does not argue that works are without value or that they are not imperative, only that works play no part in personal salvation.

By isolating the meaning of Ephesians 2:8-9 from its full text, the Abandonment Clergy have produced a nation of disarmed, would-be Christian warriors who in their minds are certain that they are, by their simple proclamations of faith, heaven-bound and that their salvation cannot be lost, especially not as a consequence of their lack of righteous works or engagement in sinful practices.

The Rest of the Works Story

The faith of Christians of all mainline denominations is grounded in the belief that eternal salvation is a gift of God which cannot be earned. But we cannot afford to stop there. God mandates throughout both Testaments that those called by His name must obey His commandments with total commitment. *Thou shalt love the Lord thy God with all thy heart, and with all thy soul, and with all thy mind* (Mat. 22:37) is called *the first and great commandment* (Mat. 22:38). Obedience is works! Clearly, God assigns considerably more importance to works than much of the Abandonment Clergy.

Putting Ephesians 2:8-9 back into context may not be very popular with the Abandonment Clergy. Acknowledging that works and Christian duty go together tends to cause controversy and considerable discomfort on the reservation, perhaps even implying political involvement which, heaven forbid, might violate the fabricated, unBiblical, two-way "wall of separation."

> *Acknowledging that works and Christian duty go together tends to cause controversy and considerable discomfort on the reservation, perhaps even implying political involvement.*

What does the rest of the Ephesians passage say? Verse 10: *For we are his workmanship, created in Christ Jesus unto good works, which God hath before ordained that we should walk in them.* Far from diminishing the value and Christian imperative for works, God is saying that we were created to do good works. He also says the purpose of those works is to glorify the Father. *Let your light so shine before men, that they may see your good works, and glorify your Father which is in heaven* (Mat. 5:16).

If the contemporary clergyman denies the importance of works, he also denies the importance of glorifying the Father. His attitude is that "as long as my free, unearned salvation cannot be lost and I am guaranteed a mansion in heaven, the rest is secondary."

A person cannot earn salvation by doing works that he thinks will please God. The centerpiece of salvation, of becoming "born again and indwelt by the Holy Spirit," is not works but rather the heart. One cannot *earn* his way into heaven. Rather, to be born again Spiritually, he must accept Jesus Christ as his personal Lord and Savior and commit his life to Him.

When a person becomes born again, he literally undergoes a Spiritual transformation of his mind whereby he, in effect, plugs into the Source of truth through the Holy Spirit, Who, revealing the will of God, will become his Source of strength, courage, Biblical wisdom, vision and power. The transformation is all-encompassing.

> *And be not conformed to this world: but be ye transformed by the renewing of your mind, that ye may prove what is that good, and acceptable, and perfect will, of God"* (Rom. 12:2). *If any man be in Christ, he is a new creature: old things are passed away; behold all things are become new. And all things are of God* (II Cor. 5:17-18).

Then the mighty works which God commands can be put into action with total obedience. *Call unto me, and I will answer thee, and show thee great and mighty things, which thou knowest not* (Jer. 33:3). The Bible claims that God is directly accessible through prayer, that He answers prayer and through the Holy Spirit will give His people the power to be triumphant over their adversaries if their actions and objectives will glorify the Father. *Greater is he that is in you, than he that is in the world* (I John 4:4).

To the born-again Christian the above will make eminent sense; to others it may seem like foolishness. But it describes the Founding Fathers and the colonists in the days of the Revolution. God answered their prayers, interceded on their behalf in otherwise hopeless situations, granted them seemingly impossible military victories and through them founded our American Republic on Christianity whereby it became recognized as the "wonder of the world."

God's principles concerning freedom and how to maintain it transcend the ages. Settings and circumstances change, but the laws of God do not. If the American people will turn back to God and obey Him, a rebirth of our nation can be achieved. We are born unto good works, even mighty works. With the Source of Spiritual light and Spiritual power we will possess the kind of discernment and wisdom essential to our total commitment to the task. The battle between freedom and tyranny is spiritual, not secular, in its essence. *For we wrestle not against flesh and blood, but against principalities, against powers, against the rulers of the darkness of this world, against spiritual wickedness in high places* (Eph. 6:12).

God Sets the Order of Priorities

The first priority God sets is faith which is followed by a natural outflowing of works. In other words first comes salvation with the transformation of one's mind. Then comes the evidence of total commitment to Jesus Christ - the works which we were born to do but could not do by our own wisdom and strength. James asks, *What doth it profit, my brethren, though a man say he hath faith, and have not works? can faith save him?* (Jas. 2:14).

But wilt thou know, O vain man, that faith without works is dead? (Jas. 2:20). James is talking about the patronizing, professing Christian who thinks he has a highway to heaven based on an out-of-context concept of "salvation without responsibility." If a man is truly born again and filled with the Holy Spirit, he will have an irresistible desire to do works that glorify God. James is saying that it is not possible to be truly plugged into the power Source and stand neutral, that good works are the evidence of one's transformation, that a mere proclamation of faith which is destitute of its outflowing evidence is no faith at all, and John claims that such a person is not of God.

> *Whosoever doeth not righteousness is not of God,* ...(I John 3:10)

This issue has been debated for decades and has been a major cause of the deadly paralysis of the vigilant dimension of our faith in confronting, turning back and destroying the works of Satan. But the Scriptures are clear regarding the importance of obedience:

> *And now... the ax is laid unto the root of the trees: therefore every tree which bringeth not forth good fruit is hewn down, and cast into the fire* (Mat. 3:10).

> *If the salt has lost its savour, it is henceforth good for nothing, but to be cast out, and to be trodden under foot of men* (Mat. 5:13). Note: Christ is calling for unrelenting vigilance. The "foot of men" means enslavement under tyranny.

> *So then because thou art lukewarm ... I will spue thee out of my mouth* (Rev. 3:16).

Tough words, aren't they? Clearly, the God of the Bible's Testaments is a demanding taskmaster, but why? If God truly loves us so much that He even sent His own

Son to die on the cross for us, why does He make such stringent demands upon the faithful that we obey Him with total commitment, even threatening to "spue us out of His mouth" if we do not?

Jesus Himself answers when He says:

Wide is the gate, and broad is the way, that leadeth to destruction, and many there be that go therein. Because strait is the gate, and narrow is the way, which leadeth unto life, and few there be that find it (Mat. 7:13-14).

Obedience is "tough love" in one sense because it is so demanding of loyalty. On the other hand, God's tough love is true love because He knows the level of obedience required if we are to be free from the yoke and tyranny of spiritual and political bondage to enjoy His blessings. There can be no "lukewarm" commitment of a Christian because total commitment is required if we are to be victorious over our merciless and relentless adversary, Satan.

America is the product of a citizenry, clergy and an association of Founding Fathers united as Christians in absolute obedience to God. They knew the total commitment which would be required of them to be victorious in Christ's cause of liberty, and to that end the Fathers committed "their lives, their fortunes and their sacred honor."

Many paid the ultimate penalty. Some died of torture, others of stress and hardship from the rigors of the war, others once wealthy died in poverty. But they selflessly did the will of God and gave us America. It takes such warriors - born-again Christians filled with life, truth and God-given power - to be victorious over the relentless wickedness of evil and achieve the blessings of liberty:

I give to you power to tread on serpents ... and over all the power of the enemy (Luke 10:19).

What is God's reaction toward those Christians who stand neutral in the holocaust and to the clergy who lead them into disobedience of His commandments? We don't need to speculate: *Woe be unto the pastors that destroy and scatter the sheep of my pasture! saith the Lord* (Jer. 23:1).

It is clear what the pastors have done against the cause of Christ by preaching only the compassionate, charitable side of "love" and deleting its action dimension. Love is obedience to the commandments which through the power of salvation produces works which call forth the vigilance and greatness in every true Christian and commits him to the battlefront. Remember, Christ came to *destroy the works of the devil* (I John 3:8), and *to set at liberty them that are oppressed* (Luke 4:18).

Situational ethics and secular considerations that would likely be the guideposts for well-meaning but unsaved Americans could never produce the loyalty, the focus, the recognized Source of authority, discernment and the solidarity of purpose essential for victory in this spiritual war. God's commandments are designed for and directed to Spiritually empowered believers whose obedience is selflessly driven by their passion to serve Him and do great and mighty works which will glorify Him. In return He promises us the blessings of liberty in all of its Spiritual and political forms.

> *God's commandments are designed for and directed to Spiritually empowered believers whose obedience is selflessly driven by their passion to serve Him and do great and mighty works which will glorify Him.*

Conclusion of Salvation and Works

Not only are "works" of central and vital importance to our faithful execution of our Christian duty, but God set a standard of righteous works that could not possibly be envisioned or achieved through the power of mortal man. In fact His standards and demands are so high that only the indwelling Holy Spirit empowering man can enable him to meet the test of works that will achieve God's purpose and grant the freedoms and blessings that we in America enjoy.

Such Spiritual empowerment is necessary because the ongoing war between righteousness and evil is spiritual, and mere secular man devoid of the Spirit and power of God stands no chance against the deceitful, enslaving spirit of Satan. Neither is he capable, when operating alone without the Holy Spirit, of achieving long-lasting political freedom of which God is the Author, or even of maintaining it. This is America's plight today in the wake of her desertion and abandonment of God under the leadership of the Abandonment Clergy.

God doesn't condition salvation upon good works. Unregenerate man is not even capable of comprehending what will please God, and so the first priority is the "transformation" of one's mind. That's why salvation is free and cannot be earned by works. Man's works, conceived by man's finite standards, are meaningless to God.

> *And be not conformed to this world, but be ye transformed by the renewing of your mind, that ye may prove what is that good, and acceptable, and perfect will, of God* (Rom. 12:2).

Please note: Although that verse is an invitation to salvation, there is not one word in it that diminishes the importance of or imperative for good works. It is in fact offering the only way by which we may know the "perfect will of God" for us inasmuch as *We are his workmanship, created in Christ Jesus unto good works,...*(Eph. 2:10). Also note that our doing "good works" is not a passive subject to Christ, not a sort of spinoff elective as the Abandonment Clergy would have us believe.

Over and again the Bible speaks of the importance God places on works. In fact the key is that if we claim to be "born again" and truly have undergone such a transforming renewal of our minds and that if we truly have, so to speak, plugged into the ultimate power Source, then the works unto which we have been created will be revealed to us according to our "calling." Such power will be given to us that *...if ye do these things, ye shall never fall* (II Pet. 1:10). If we obey God and do the things which He commands and will never fall, by what right, logic or authority can we justify, as the Abandonment Clergy do, ceasing to do as we are commanded?

How important are "works" to Christ? *...let us not love in word, neither in tongue; but in deed and in truth* (I John 3:18).

> *He that saith, I know him, and keepeth not his commandments, is a liar, and the truth is not in him* (I John 2:4).

That's about as tough a mandate regarding the imperative for works and consequence for abdication of duty as anything can be. From cover to cover, literally thousands of times, God promises to do all manner of wondrous things for us. But those promises inevitably are conditioned upon *our* taking the initiative and doing certain works that demonstrate our faith. "If you will, then I will...". *If,* with all our heart, mind and soul we want to be free and we turn to God through prayer and a pure heart, He will answer us, show us the way, grant us the power to destroy the evil works of Satan and achieve the victory which glorifies the Father. Satan is no match for a committed Christian. Without the power of Christ, man is no match for Satan.

God sent His only begotten Son to show us the way to Spiritual and political freedom and to give His life in that cause. How important, then, would you say "works" are to God? Get an excellent Bible concordance such as *Strongs* and look up "works." You will be astounded.

Works are essential to freedom. They are the essence of obedience to the commandments. *Fear God, and keep his commandments: for this is the whole duty of man* (Eccl. 12:13).

Obedience, that is, "works," is therefore not an elective. The Abandonment Clergy, who preach salvation out of the context of the great and mighty works of righteousness that God declares

> *Obedience, that is, "works," is therefore not an elective.*

will flow from it, teach a false doctrine. It mocks God, and God will not be mocked. These clergy, in full defiance of God's clear mandates to works and action, betray Christ, our country (which is of Him) and our children. Christianity is a faith which calls its adherents to the highest commitment to duty, responsibility and greatness. It gives them the knowledge, wisdom, vision, direction and power essential to victory over the deceit, slavery and death brought by Satan.

As an aside, the God-given freedoms we in America enjoy have their roots in the Constitution which itself is founded upon the Biblical laws of God. The Constitution was designed to be the servant of the citizens; thus the Preamble opens with "We the People..." The Constitution presupposes that the citizens will demonstrate the highest level of responsibility (works) toward their political representatives and will govern their own lives (works) by the highest moral code of the Bible, beginning with the Ten Commandments. As the citizens become passive under a pretense that "God is in control so it doesn't matter anyway," they cease to be *salt* (Mat. 5:13) and *light* (Mat. 5:16). Both being forms of "works," God's response will be that they are *thenceforth good for nothing but to be cast out and to be trodden under the foot of men* (Mat. 5:13). That is, they will lose their liberties and become enslaved under tyrants governed by their own fallen human nature.

Those who think the clergy preaching Abandonment Theology are right in offering a free, out-of-context salvation from which no duties, responsibilities or Spiritual empowerment can be expected to flow, should reexamine that thesis. Christ gave His life, and he told believers: *Take up* [your] *cross and follow me* (Mat. 16:24). That is a mandate calling Christians to the highest and most sacrificial standards of duty and works. It is what is required of the citizens of America if our God-given Constitution is to remain powerful and a light of hope to the world.

> *It takes such warriors - born-again Christians filled with Life, truth and power - to be victorious over the relentless wickedness of evil, and to achieve and maintain the blessings of liberty.*

God doesn't require that we do works as a condition of salvation. Why should He? Unsaved man cannot comprehend the truth and works of God. *...all our righteousnesses are as filthy rags* (Isa. 64:6). Conversely, works founded upon God's revealed truth and empowered by the Holy Spirit will possess a conquering power that can *...destroy the works of the devil* (I John 3:8).

God's message is clear: We are born unto good works, but until we have been "born again" we are not capable of understanding them, nor will we have the necessary Spiritual power to do them. Therefore, salvation cannot be earned; *it is the gift of God* (Eph. 2:8) that must be intensely desired by an individual and requested of God. It is between God and one's heart, devoid of works, because no works by unregenerate man can meet God's standards. Period!

The Abandonment Clergy and all clergy should be teaching that salvation cannot be earned and it is unmerited inasmuch as we *all have sinned and come short of the glory of God* (Rom. 3:23). True salvation is a transforming process from which we can expect to receive from God revelations of His truth and of our responsibilities and duties to Him as they pertain to works and action in the cause of Christ.

> *"Born-again" means transformed and empowered by the now-indwelling Holy Spirit, so that we may faithfully and decisively serve in God's army and do those mighty works of righteousness against which the darkness and evil of Satan cannot prevail.*

Salvation and outflowing works are inseparable. It is a matter of cause and effect. James laid it on the line: *Be ye doers of the word, and not hearers only, deceiving your own selves* (Jas. 1:22). James continued: *Even so faith, if it hath not works, is dead, being alone* (Jas. 2:17).

James is saying that a profession of faith cannot stand alone without the outflowing evidence of the transformed condition of your mind. "Born-again" means transformed and empowered by the now-indwelling Holy Spirit so that we may faithfully and decisively serve in God's army and do those mighty works of righteousness against which the darkness and evil of Satan cannot prevail.

That was the faith of the Founding Fathers through which America was born. The converse is that the Abandonment Clergy are by default surrendering our liberties to the tyranny of Satan.

Romans 13:1-4: Is God in Control of Our Government?

Is it an expression of true Christian faith to proclaim, "God is in control of our government. Don't be concerned," and then to walk away from any sense of responsibility? If God is in control, what is the duty of the Christian citizen? If Satan is in control, what must the Christian citizen do?

For centuries these questions have plagued Christians and the clergy the world over. The wrong answers opened the floodgates in pre-Nazi Germany to Hitler.

In recent decades Romans 13:1 and 2 have been taken out of their Biblical context by America's clergy. The consequence is that the verses' meaning has been inverted from God's intent, resulting in terrible confusion and non-involvement of the very people charged by God with the maintenance of freedom.

> *Let every soul be subject unto the higher powers. For there is no power but of God: the powers that be are ordained of God* (Rom. 13:1).

> *Whosoever therefore resisteth the power* [defined in verse 1 as government, or rulers - ed.], *resisteth the ordinance of God: and they that resist shall receive to themselves damnation* (Rom. 13:2).

These two verses appear to say that government is God's business, not ours, so no matter what happens we should leave it in God's hands. Further, God seems to be saying that if we resist our republic's slide into corruption and evil, we Christians will bring damnation upon ourselves.

Is God, in the matter of government, contradicting His calls throughout the Scriptures to our total commitment in His cause of righteousness, His mandates that we be *salt* and *light,* and *bold as a lion* (in confronting evil), that we *occupy,* and *stand up for* [Him] *against the workers of iniquity?* In verse 2 is God establishing a double standard by declaring government to be off limits for Christians?

If so, what has happened? Beginning with the founding of our Constitutional Republic and continuing for almost two centuries, all American citizens, including the Congress and President of the United States, were taught by their churches, schools and colleges that it was their sacred duty to defend the Constitution, the very centerpiece of our government, which itself defines and makes possible our God-given liberties.

That has now changed.

Therefore, as Christians, how involved in the political process are we to be? Or are we to be involved in the political process at all? Are we to live virtuously and obey God in all of personal life but stay out of politics? If so, why did God grant victory to George Washington and the colonies against impossible military odds in the War for Independence, thus establishing a nation

> *In pre-Nazi Germany the clergy acknowledged God's control, but they misinterpreted Romans 13:1 and 2 to mean that the fate of Germany was in God's hands, not theirs.*

whose people have been blessed beyond any in recorded history?

Is God in control of governments, or isn't He?

In pre-Nazi Germany the clergy acknowledged God's control, but they misinterpreted Romans 13:1 and 2 to mean that the fate of Germany was in God's hands, not theirs. Thus, they withdrew their leadership on the great freedom issues of the day even though those issues are addressed in the Bible. They saw the approaching evil but went silent, rationalizing that God knew what He was doing, and they were not to interfere. Their followers were left Spiritually leaderless. Great confusion set in, and the people became easy victims of Hitler.

Hitler saw what was happening. He recognized the resulting weakness and irresolution of the people as the clergy abandoned their sacred duty to be *watchmen* (Ezekiel 33:6) and to blow the trumpet, and warn the people (See Eze. 33:3). He wrote about it in *Mein Kampf.*

> One of the worst symptoms of decay was the increasing cowardice toward responsibility as well as the half-heartedness in all things resulting from it....Everywhere one began to evade responsibility and for this reason one preferred to take up half and insufficient measures....[113]

> All these symptoms of decay were ultimately only consequences of the lack of a certain, commonly acknowledged view of life and of the general uncertainty in the judgment, and the definition of an attitude towards the various great questions of the time, resulting from it. Therefore, everything, beginning with education, is half-hearted and wavering, shuns responsibility and ends thus in cowardly tolerance of even recognized evils. [114]

Does this sound alarmingly parallel to conditions in America today? Clearly, Germany - and the world - paid a horrible price as a consequence of Germany's Abandonment Clergy.

Closer to home, sparked by a dissenting opinion in the 1947 U.S. Supreme Court case *Everson v. Board of Education,* America's Abandonment Clergy and their followers allowed the Supreme Court to deliberately erect an unprecedented two-way "wall of separation" between church and state. This was in blatant defiance of our nation's Christian founding and tradition.

A critical turning point then came in 1962 in the landmark case of *Engel v. Vitale,* when the Abandonment Clergy and their followers allowed God to be expelled from the public schools. In the opinion of the Chief Justice of the New York Court of Appeals:

> ...such a holding would destroy a part of the essential foundation of the American govern-mental structure.[115]

A series of reaffirming U.S. Supreme Court cases followed, and in 1980 the Court found it "unconstitutional for the Ten Commandments to hang on the walls of a classroom..." *(Stone v. Graham).*[116]

Clearly, these cases demonstrated a consistent intent to expel the influence of God - and with it the knowledge and awareness of America's Biblical heritage - from the minds of her youth, her future leaders.

Without this knowledge of the Source and foundation of their God-given freedoms and of their God-mandated duties, an open door to total power of the government would result. Misapplying Romans 13:1 and 2 out of context, the Abandonment Clergy refused to become involved in what they termed "political" issues such as the above cases. Thus they withdrew their leadership in what was most clearly a Biblical issue.

What is the correct interpretation of Romans 13:1 and 2? To understand their meaning, it is necessary to place them in context with verses 3 and 4:

> *(1) Let every soul be subject unto the higher powers. For there is no power but of God: the powers that be are ordained of God.*

(2) Whosoever therefore resisteth the power, resisteth the ordinance of God: and they that resist shall receive to themselves damnation.

(3) For rulers are not a terror to good works, but to evil. Wilt thou then not be afraid of the power? do that which is good, and thou shalt have praise of the same:

(4) For he [the government - ed] *is the minister of God to thee for good. But if thou do that which is evil, be afraid; for he beareth not the sword in vain: for he is the minister of God, a revenger to execute wrath upon him that doeth evil.*

Please note that sentences beginning with the word "for" are meant to define and explain that which came before. Thus verses 1 and 2 without their defining 3 and 4 are misleading.

By taking verse 1 out of context, the Abandonment Clergy declare that God has ordained and is in control of all governments - both good and evil - and that the duty of a Christian citizen in being subordinate to God is to offer no resistance to government. Could this be God's will, even when the government is clearly becoming corrupted and is descending into a rulership of evil men?

This misinterpretation also provides the Abandonment Clergy with false support for the two-way "wall of separation" between church and state, exposed in Chapter Two of this book for the affront that it is to the unquestionable intent of the Founding Fathers.

Verses 1 and 2, standing alone, have long been used to confuse and neutralize millions of otherwise faithful Christians who, if they knew the truth about their duties, would without hesitation answer God's call to be *salt* and *light* in their government, national, state and local. In the state and national political arenas, these Christians would become formidable adversaries to today's pervasive godlessness among our elected representatives, or "rulers."

Romans 13:3 states that the purpose of government under God is to be a terror to evil and to advance good works. "Good works" in that context means works under the authority of God; thus they are the liberating works of His righteousness, the fountainhead of our personal and civil liberties.

Verse 3 concludes with the mandate that we *do that which is good, and thou shalt have praise of the same.* That is, we as citizens must live by God's laws and ordinances of righteousness, live up to our responsibilities and our sacred duties. That commitment, which often requires maximum vigilance, is our mandate from God.

In exchange for our Founding Fathers,' clergy's and colonists' faithful obedience to God when America was founded, He poured out upon her citizens - then and for generations to come - His blessings of freedom, prosperity and happiness. Our nation became a mighty fortress - a torch of freedom in spirit and in power.

God charged the people with the sacred duty to watch over their

> *In exchange for our Founding Fathers,' clergy's and colonists' faithful obedience to God when America was founded, He poured out upon her citizens - then and for generations to come - His blessings of freedom, prosperity and happiness.*

government and politicians - to be certain they perform their duties in accordance with His ordinances as set forth in the Scriptures. The citizens, therefore, hold the ultimate responsibility for the operations of their government.

Romans 13:4 reconfirms verse 3 and in positive terms establishes God's purpose for government: *For he* [government-ed.] *is a minister to thee for good.* What is "good"? God is good; thus "good" is righteousness. That is, the government of God is a government founded upon His laws and ordinances of righteousness, from which count-less blessings flow to the citizens. Such a government is the archenemy of a government of Satan, who came ...*to steal, and to kill, and to destroy* (John 10:10).

Next, verse 4 denounces evil as the adversary of God's government and empowers the government to purge itself of evil: *But if thou doeth that which is evil, be afraid; for he* [government] *beareth not the sword in vain: for he is a minister of God, a revenger to execute wrath upon him that doeth evil.*

Bear in mind that God established our Constitu-tional government to be the servant of the citizens (totally unique in the history of governments) and gave the citizens the Divine charge to rule over our gov-ernment accord-ing to His laws of righteousness set forth in the Bible (See Ch. 1). It is thus impossible for America's Christian citizens to live in obedi-ence to God and to simultaneously abdicate their respon-sibilities in the affairs of government.

> *God's government, our Constitu-tional Republic, was designed by the Founding Fathers to be invin-cible to external and internal threats only so long as the citizens and their political representatives remain righteous, God-fearing and a terror to any evil adversary.*

God's government, our Constitutional Republic, was designed by the Founding Fathers to be invincible to external and internal threats only so long as the citizens and their political representatives remain righteous, God-fearing and a terror to any evil adversary.

Ours is a government "of the people, by the people, and for the people." God designed it that way - to be the servant of the people, not the reverse (See Ch. 1). The mandate of God to America's citizens is therefore that of total involvement in the affairs of our government.

Back to the question: *Is* God in control of our government and all other governments?

The answer is a resounding *Yes!* But God is not evil. Satan is evil. A corrupted government is not a government of God, but of Satan.

In fact, history records that Germany's Nazi government became made up of demonized, anti-Christian cultists and satanists. Many of the Christian clergy were exterminated in Hitler's death camps.

And *yes* - God was at all times in control of Germany's Nazi government, but Satan was orchestrating it. God has made it clear throughout the Scriptures that if His people disobey Him and fall away from their faith, He will allow the entrance of Satan and the travesties which come with him.

And *yes* - God is today in control of our government. He has the power to intervene, to override the works of Satan. But He is quite clear in stating in the Scriptures that although He has that power and authority, He will not use it in the face of an abandoning, defiant people. To the extent that we abandon Him, He will abandon us by opening the floodgates to judgment through Satan. That's what the Book of Deuteronomy is all about with its vivid descriptions of blessings and consequences.

God did not abdicate His throne over Nazi Germany nor has He abdicated His throne today over the United States or the world. He gave the German people, as He gives us today, the blessing of volition, the right to choose between Him and Satan - between righteousness and evil.

> *I have set before you life and death, blessing and cursing; therefore choose life, that both you and your seed* [children-ed.] *may live* (Deut.31:19).

Citizen Involvement in Government - How Far?

The very spirit and strength of our Bible-based American Constitutional Republic is that of the citizens' total involvement in the affairs of government. A Bible-based citizenry must understand that their God-ordained duty, in return for their God-given freedoms, is to assure that all politicians, including the Congress, the President and his appointees such as Supreme Court justices right down to the state and local levels, perform their duties in accordance with the civil and moral codes of God upon which our republic rests.

Revolution is not the way of God to solve America's crises today. On the contrary, total involvement in the political process, with the Bible as the standard, is the way of God. That's why He gave us a Constitutional Republic within which to work and to perform our sacred citizenship duties.

Nowhere in the Bible does God call for or sanction our abandonment of duty in the affairs of government. He does not draw the line of responsibility.

America's Christians need to: (1) put Romans 1-4 together in context; (2) change their roles from being confused, misled spectators of the decline of our republic; and (3) get back to the battlefronts where God commands them to be and, knowing the truth, where they would want to be. We must take the initiative, bearing in mind that through the Holy Spirit we hold the ultimate power to restore what we have been given. These are times that demand the best we have to offer - the greatness that God has placed in every person.

Satan's Strategy and Triumphs

Satan knows that committed Christians possess a Spiritual power over which he cannot prevail. If we resist the devil, he will flee from us (See Jas. 4:7). Darkness hates the Light and will do everything possible to extinguish it. Satan cannot accomplish that task by head-on confrontation; thus he must operate by stealth and deception whereby the desensitized, undiscerning people surrender their God-given freedoms piecemeal through a process of erosion until suddenly they wake up and realize that they are defenseless before Satan's conquering barbarians.

The Christian culture of our God-given free country is being eradicated. Christ, the Author of our freedoms, the "Light of the world," is being outlawed while Satan's darkness and tyranny are being legalized.

Following are just a few examples of the result of Satan's strategies for breaking America's Spiritual back. He has seduced a once great, God-fearing people into abandoning the militant, action-based dimension of their faith and its application to the perpetuation of freedom without even realizing they are doing so. He is breaking down America's Spiritual and military defenses and imperiling her freedoms which would have been impossible to accomplish without the aid of the Abandonment Theologians.

What has Satan already accomplished in America? Evidence of his deceitful tactics is easy to find. For example, whereas America funds 85% of the world's missionaries, where does this money come from? It comes from you and me, from our Christian generosity and a longing to see other peoples in the world living in the light of Christ, free to worship and free from suffering under the darkness of tyranny and oppression.

But Satan has convinced many that "money is the root of all evil." This contention opposes free enterprise and is the basis for socialism. It is a distortion of the Scriptures which proclaim that it is the *love of money* that is the root of all evil (See I Tim. 6:10).

Money is a powerful servant if kept in proper perspective. However, when money becomes an end in itself and God takes second place, then money will have become an idol that God will not tolerate: *Thou shalt have no other gods before me* (Ex. 20:3 - the first of the Ten Commandments).

When idolatry in any form comes between America's Christians and God, it costs us our freedoms. As the people lose their focus on the righteousness of God, gradually they will become *trees without fruit* (Jude 12), *wells without water* (II Pet. 2:17), and *clouds without water* (Jude 12).

The distorted notion that "money is the root of all evil" ignores the fact that God gave us our free enterprise, profit-based economic system. It is this system which gives us the power for financial stewardship by which we fund those missionary efforts throughout the world in obedience to "The Great Commission." Such application of a percentage of our wealth, our profits (which are themselves often a measure of what we have done for others), is stewardship at its noblest level. Those who are in poverty and suffering under the boot of tyranny are not likely to be in a position to exercise effective economic stewardship.

A transition to a socialist economy (into which our nation is plunging) will bring enslavement without freedom to worship, an end to stewardship in His cause and an end to God's blessings of liberty. Hitler, Marx, Mao, Gorbachev, Yeltsin - all were or are socialists. It stands to reason that the Abandonment Clergy should challenge their ways and join the front lines of the battles to save our God-given free enterprise system rather than perpetuate this distorted thinking.

What else has Satan accomplished in America through the Abandonment Clergy and their followers? Below are summarized some areas of his deadliest influence:

(1) Works: Neutralized the will of many Christians to stand and fight for their liberties by convincing them that "works" are not important.

(2) Government: Inverted the meaning of Romans 13:1 and 2 to discourage Christian involvement and exercise of their sacred duties in the affairs of government.

(3) Outlawed God in the public schools: Abraham Lincoln agreed with our Founding Fathers that America's future security rested in teaching children the highest Biblical and moral principles. He understood the consequences of denying them that heritage. He said, "The philosophy of the schoolroom in one generation will be the philosophy of government in the next."[117] It follows that the vacuum created by removing God from the schools invited an invasion of the "anything but Jesus" cults. For example, when in 1962 God was ousted from the classroom, witchcraft among our youth was almost unheard of. Today it is a national epidemic. Much of this book concerns the freedom-endangering consequences to the American people after they allowed God to be expelled from the public schools.

(4) Two-way "wall of separation": The fabrication of a two-way wall between church and state making it illegal for the church to intrude in the affairs of the state. Such a barrier is an open-door license for political representatives to conduct themselves according to their sinful fallen nature, which manifests itself through all manner of debased, immoral conduct and a loss of Biblical perspective in the commission of their duties. It also confuses and thus partly disables the citizens, making them unable to effectively conduct their sacred responsibilities in demanding the highest Bible-based moral conduct from their legislators and other representatives.

(5) Love: Trivializing of the faith by inverting "love" from an action mandate for obedience to the Commandments to a sentiment primarily of charity and tolerance. Love, in its full dimension, is the most action-based expression in the Bible. To water it down so it becomes simply a turn-the-other-cheek justification for tolerance of evil is to extract the teeth from our faith.

(6) "End-times, last days": Overuse of eschatology (the study of future events), Biblical prophecy and apparent signs of the times generates an abdication of duty, futility, despair and an attitude of "Why bother?" It encourages Christians to slacken their resolve to obey Christ's mandate to "occupy" until He returns, [the Second Coming], and thus by default encourages the onslaught of the forces which would destroy America's freedoms.

(7) Homosexuality: This practice is condemned by God as "abomination," "unclean" (transmitters for death-dealing diseases such as AIDS; "dishonorable," "vile," "against nature," not genetic, not an "alternate liftstyle"). Sodomy laws forbidding homosexuals in the military since the founding of America are now being compromised by the President and Congress and given respect in society in general. Church denominations ordain homosexual ministers in defiance of God's injunction while the majority of Christians passively consent to this mockery of God Whose wrath it invites.

(8) Women (wives, mothers, daughters) in combat: Women in combat is another "abomination" condemned by God. It is an inversion of the "natural" role for which God created women and leads to the destruction of a nation through downgrading and demoralizing its military combat forces (See Chapter **4**).

(9) Abortion: This legalized murder of innocent children in their mother's wombs is called "termination of unviable or unwanted 'tissue' or 'fetus.'" Such tragedy has spawned the expression, "The most dangerous place in America today is in a mother's womb." This murder of infants would be expected in the Nazi death camps but not in Christian America, especially not under the banner of the mother's "choice." Her choice should be made before conception when there is only one life involved, not afterward when there are two. The baby's DNA is not the mother's DNA. The child is not part of her. Mother and child are entirely different people. The mother is responsible before God for the child.

The ultimate mockery of God has been the legalizing of partial-birth abortions. In this form of abortion the child can be 95% born. There the birth is stopped, and the doctor murders the infant with a process of unspeakable cruelty. A nation that tolerates the murder of its children as a form of birth control mocks God, Who condemns the "taking of innocent blood."

(10) "Peace, peace; when there is no peace": Years of disarming, neutralizing propaganda take the fight out of Christians. The claim ignores "fallen human nature" and God's mandates for vigilance by selling the false doctrine of "peace" or "peace in our time" or "peaceful coexistence" (with evil governments) as if peace were nothing more than the absence of battlefield conflict. *And from the prophet even unto the priest every one dealeth falsely...saying, Peace, peace; when there is no peace* (Jer. 6:13-14).

The doctrine of "peace in our time" has been a cruel hoax upon the American people, long perpetuated by the

U.S. government and the Abandonment Clergy who ignored and compromised God's many warnings. This resulted in the people's acceptance of freedom-endangering policies of unilateral military disarmament in the face of massive nuclear proliferation and weapons development and stockpiling by America's enemies (See Chapter 3).

Conclusion: The Curse of Toleration and Compromise

The above are some, but by no means all, of the spheres of Satan's influence which is all-pervasive. He is a master of deceit; his cruelty knows no bounds. He is spirit and is alive and intensely active. He is a destroyer of life and liberty. The only effective defense against Satan is Jesus Christ, the Author of liberty and the Giver of life. There can be no compromise of loyalty to Christ or of vigilance in obedience to Him by those who would defend and perpetuate to posterity the blessings of God's liberty.

Question: What do all of the above travesties have in common? What is their common denominator - the thread which is leading to the death of America and the enslavement of our children?

Answer: It is tolerance and compromise - tolerance of and compromise with evil. Such tolerance in any degree is compromise with God's laws of righteousness. That's like tolerance for just a little malignant cancer. Compromise is impossible, and death will surely follow. There must be only one conduct in our relationship to evil: like malignant cancer it must be totally cut out. Such intolerance is anathema to the Abandonment Clergy because by definition Abandonment is tolerance for evil by backing away from absolute commitment to the righteousness of God.

Thus compromise has brought upon America the legitimizing of homosexuality, which God terms "abomination," which is unleashed on society, onto our children and now onto our military forces. The murder of our children at birth is sanctioned by a compromising Abandonment Clergy and nation of their compromising Christian followers. The compromising, tolerant clergy allow the expulsion of God from the classroom and the erection of a fabricated two-way wall of separation between church and state.

The tolerant, compromising Abandonment Clergy are leading our nation to its destruction, and the task ahead for the "remnant" is clear.

The Most Intolerant Man

Jesus Christ never tolerated evil. He confronted it and exposed it. In that sense it could be said that Jesus was the most intolerant man who ever walked on planet earth. He never once compromised God's laws of righteousness. If America is to be saved, we, like Christ, must be intolerant of any compromise with His laws.

CHAPTER SEVEN

DISCOVERING BIBLICAL SOLUTIONS

I have set before you life and death, blessing and cursing:
therefore choose life, that both you and your children may live.
Deuteronomy 30:19

Responsibility for Abandonment and for Revival

Two basic explanations exist for this surge of abandonment. One, someone has taken an active role. Two, someone else has taken an inactive role. In reality, the responsibility lies as heavily on those who *let it happen* as it does with those who *make it happen*.

So who is letting this happen? America's clergy, for one. Slowly, step by step, those charged with keeping the people ever mindful of God's Word as it applies to the sacred cause of liberty have dropped their banner of vigilance and duty, preaching a modernized "social gospel." America's youth have been abandoned by their clergy and their unsuspecting parents. A handful of Patrick Henry-type clergy and Christian patriots throughout the nation have been sounding the alarm, publishing warnings and trying to reach people through radio and television. But they have been scorned by the Abandonment Clergy and their victimized followers, labeled "extremists" and ridiculed into impotence. The clergy retreated to the financially profitable, politically neutral social reservation, creating a vacuum which the foes of America's freedoms rushed in to fill.

151

All Citizens, Especially America's Christians

Every citizen who is a beneficiary of America's freedoms, especially the freedom to worship as he or she pleases - or not to worship at all - has a duty to defend the Judeo-Christian pillars and laws of our nation that make such freedom possible. In no sense is this duty a compromise with one's own religious convictions. In America this duty simply guarantees a person's right to worship as he pleases without fear of persecution.

By now Christians should realize that they have the primary responsibility for reclaiming our nation's Christian heritage because it is Christianity upon which the Declaration of Independence and the Constitution were founded.

In addition, Biblical Christians are - or should be - bound together as were those in colonial

> *Biblical Christians are bound together, as were those in colonial days, in the belief and conviction that the inerrant, infallible Word of God is the final authority on all matters personal and civil.*

days in the belief and conviction that the inerrant, infallible Word of God is the final authority on all matters personal and civil. It was that conviction by the clergy, the citizens and the Fathers which miraculously produced this oasis called America. Christianity worked. Throughout history nothing else worked to liberate and free the individual citizen.

This country was not founded by Hindus, Muslims, deists or followers of any other religion. It was founded by a nation of committed Christians bound together by their common belief in the Trinity - Father, Son and Holy Spirit - and their belief that Biblical doctrine applies to every facet of temporal life. Many denominations argued about superficial variations, but they were consolidated as a mighty force in their Christian Worldview.

All believed in the transforming power of Jesus Christ, in salvation as a gift of God. They also believed that the power of the Holy Spirit dwelling in a born-again Christian is evidenced by an outflowing of mighty works. These Christians believed that God was directly accessible through prayer and that He would intercede and grant miraculous victories out of otherwise seemingly hopeless circumstances.

In fact both the colonists and the British declared that God's personal intervention in response to the prayers of General George Washington, his soldiers, the Congress, the clergy and three million American Christian citizens is the only possible explanation of why the Revolution was a triumph. Our hope for America today can be found in our heritage of yesterday, in the invincible nature of true born-again Christians joined in battle, applying their ability to discern truth from error and right from wrong. A rebirth of that fire will prevail against the works of the devil, who has come *to steal, to kill, and to destroy* (John 10:10).

A Jewish-American Revolutionary

Although America was not founded upon Judaism, the Christian faith is founded upon Judaism and the Old Testament. Judaism speaks of the same God, the same Ten Commandments, the same duties to obey Him and His Commandments and of the same freedoms.

How did the Jews living at the time of the Christian American Revolution feel about supporting it? The answer is found in the little-known story of George Washington's banker, a Jew named Haym Salomon.

In the most desperate hours of the American Revolution when the Congress was out of money to supply weapons and provisions to the militia, Philadelphia Jewish banker, Haym Salomon, answered the call for help. Salomon, because of the persecution that his relatives and friends had endured in Europe, believed so strongly in America's cause of freedom that he committed his personal fortune and appealed to the Jews of both America and Europe for financing. They responded by lending millions of dollars to the Continental Congress *without note or interest.* Salomon became known as "The Financier of The Revolution."[118]

Salomon was a committed orthodox Jew. He recognized that central to the Christian War for Independence was the conviction that it was God's will that people be free to worship according to their own faith. The Christian institutions which were the foundations and guarantors of such unprecedented rights were worth fighting for and defending. Jews throughout America and the world agreed and generously contributed of their resources.

The Founding Fathers made it clear that the Christian pillars of liberty allowed for previously unknown freedom of worship. In exchange for those freedoms, it became every citizen's duty to fight for the preservation of those institutions which are the fountainhead of the countless blessings which all Americans and future generations would enjoy.

It is *not* a non-Christian's obligation to adopt or convert to the Christian faith. But it *is* the duty of every American citizen to defend the Constitution and the Judeo-Christian pillars of law and liberty which grant us such freedoms.

Haym Salomon had given all Americans a shining example of setting priorities. It is true that American citizens represent a melting pot of different cultures and religions, and we are all Americans living under a system which, properly maintained, will guarantee life, liberty and the pursuit of happiness. That, as Salomon rightly concluded, is our common cause. Regardless of citizens' personal religions, the freedoms we enjoy are founded upon the Old and New Testaments. It is our obligation and duty to do all in our power to defend them.

Maintaining Freedom: Whose Responsibility?

So what can we actually do? Great numbers of well-meaning Christians throughout America are frustrated today over national and world conditions. They're confused about the crucial life-and-death freedom issues. This has happened because knowledge of their heritage, beginning in the pulpit and extending into education, has been all but erased. The resulting confusion has been neutralizing Christians into inactivity in areas of their faith where there can be no substitute for action.

Heaven forbid that Reverend R.C. Sproul may be proved right in his charge that "the narcotic effect of ecclesiastical opium" has rendered America's Christians so impotent that "the church's extinction will come not by sword or pillory but by the quiet death of irrelevance. It will pass away with a whimper not a bang."[119] The Founding Fathers would be not only alarmed but angry and distraught to learn how little we are doing to reclaim our heritage.

Remember what we used to have? In 1892 the United States Supreme Court made an exhaustive study of the supposed connection between Christianity and the American Constitutional Republic. The Court's finding, mentioned in Chapter 1, merits repeating. After reviewing hundreds of historical documents, the Court asserted:

> Our laws and our institutions must necessarily
> be based upon and embody the teachings of the

Redeemer of mankind. It is impossible that it
should be otherwise; and in this sense and to
this extent our civilization and our institutions
are emphatically Christian.... This is a religious
people. This is historically true. From the dis-
covery of this continent to the present hour,
there is a single voice making this affirmation....
We find everywhere a clear recognition of the
same truth.... These, and many other matters
which might be noticed, add a volume of unoffi-
cial declarations to the mass of organic utter-
ances that this is a Christian nation.[120]

These were people who obeyed and lived by the
commandments of God, Who, in turn, blessed them and
us with freedoms inconceivable and unknown in the long,
bloody, tyrannical history of the world. God honored His
promise.

> *And it shall come to pass, if thou shalt harken
> diligently unto the voice of the Lord thy God, to
> observe and to do all his commandments which
> I command thee this day, that the Lord thy God
> will set thee on high above all nations of the
> earth: And all these blessings shall come on
> thee...* (Deut. 28:1-2).

Deuteronomy was George Washington's favorite book
of the Bible. It is about building a free nation. This verse
encapsulates the steadfast faith and commitment of the
Fathers, and it is the only way that America will be saved
at this late hour. It is the core of the priceless heritage
which has been deleted in our public schools and which
must be restored.

Christians neutralized into inactivity will be spectators of their country's free fall to collapse. They will watch
as a free, sovereign, once God-fearing nation slips into a
most unhappy state in which *they that hate you shall*

reign over you (Lev. 26:17). What then, is the solution? It isn't good enough to simply say, "We have to get back to God." What specifically must the Christian and other citizens of America do?

What Christ Would Have Us Do

(1) Choose a side. *IIe that is not with me is against me* (Mat. 12:30). There can be no middle ground for a Christian charged with the defense of his nation's liberty. To triumph over Satan requires total commitment. And, yes, God has given us the gift of volition, the right of choice. *I have set before you life and death, blessing and cursing: therefore choose life, that both you and your children may live* (Deut. 30:19). Not choosing is not an option. Silence is a choice - bondage.

(2) Maintain and defend your freedom. *Stand fast in the liberty wherewith Christ hath made us free* (Gal. 5:1). First comes Spiritual freedom; then inevitably in its wake follows a great movement for political freedom. *Occupy till I come* (Luke 19:13). "Occupy" is a full-action term which calls for a full-dimensional defense against the workers of iniquity and the relentless "wiles of the devil."

(3) Verbalize boldly. *I charge thee therefore before God, and the Lord Jesus Christ,... Preach the word; be instant in season, out of season; reprove, rebuke, exhort...* (II Tim. 4:1-2). *The righteous are bold as a lion* (Prov. 28:1). *Put on the whole armour of God* (Eph. 6:11). *Take the... sword of the Spirit* (Eph. 6:17). *Go...and teach all nations* (Mat. 28:19).

(4) Join the battle. *Who will rise up for me against the evildoers? or who will stand up for me against the workers* *of iniquity?* (Ps. 94:16). This is God's roll call to the faithful, the brave and the vigilant. Throughout both Testaments, He calls the faithful into the battle.

(5) Be vigilant. *Be sober, be vigilant; because your adversary the devil, as a roaring lion, walketh about, seeking whom he may devour* (I Peter 5:8). That is, Satan never rests. He will attack any vulnerability if you let down your guard - even a little. His objective is *to steal, and to kill, and to destroy* (John 10:10) you, your family and your freedom.

(6) Do your duty. *Fear God, and keep his commandments: for this is the whole duty of man* (Eccl. 12:13). Obedience and engagement in the struggles is not an elective for a Christian. It is a duty, an obligation and a condition of the blessings of liberty. *I command thee this day to love the Lord thy God, to walk in his ways, and to keep his commandments and his statutes* (Deut. 30:16). Jesus said, *If thou wilt enter into life, keep the commandments* (Mat. 19:17). Life and liberty are directly related in the Declaration of Independence. To be free, keep the commandments.

(7) Guard your sacred trust. *O Timothy, keep that which is committed to thy trust* (I Tim. 6:20).

(8) Hate evil. *Ye that love the Lord, hate evil:* (Ps. 97:10). Is a Christian given permission to hate? A Christian is not just given permission to hate evil, he is commanded to hate it. "Hate" means to "utterly reject." Because of the Abandonment Theologians and their followers, many Christians consider "love" to be a term of tolerance that allows compromise with evil. But God is love, God is truth, and truth cannot tolerate evil. Neither can evil stand in the presence of truth. It will flee the light of Christ. America's Christians who declare their love for our country but have disengaged from the battle have probably lost their Spiritual discernment as a result of the misinterpretation of the non-compromising essence of love. To the extent of their tolerance of evil, they open the floodgates to its deadly attacks.

(9) Be "salt" and "light." *Ye are the salt of the earth... Ye are the light of the world.... Let your light so shine before men, that they may see your good works, and glorify your Father which is in heaven* (Mat. 5:13-14,16). The "Great Commission" of the Christian is that he declare the gospel of truth at every opportunity. There is power in the spoken word of truth, but it cannot be released if the Christian keeps it to himself. Satan fears and cannot stand against the truth. Thus as a general principle, "closet Christians," by withholding that power, sin by their silence.

(10) Be steadfast. *I have fought a good fight, I have finished my course, l have kept the faith* (II Tim. 4:7). Paul, like Christ, set the example for future generations. He did not say, "I retired to the social reservation." The fires of his faith and his obedience to God drove him on, and despite his terrible sufferings Paul gave the world his priceless, inspired treasures as the principal writer of the New Testament. In that same invincible faith and spirit, the Founding Fathers gave us America and triumphed over tyranny. It is with that same zeal and conviction that millions of Christians must urgently leave their reservations and bleachers, "keep the faith" and "fight a good fight," if America is to be spared and her torch of freedom passed to posterity.

These action mandates are mere samplings of the consistent call of God for eternal vigilance and total loyalty. Thus the first and great commandment states, *Thou shalt love the Lord thy God with all thy heart, and*

with all thy soul, and with all thy mind (Mat. 22:37).
Inasmuch as love is obedience, clearly God is calling for
total commitment to truth and total rejection of evil.

What If We Elect Not to Obey?

*Be not deceived God is not mocked; for whatsoever a man
soweth, that shall he also reap* (Gal. 6:7).

Of course we still have the freedom to choose. We can
choose to ignore God, or we can intentionally disobey
Him. What would happen then? The answer is not a
pleasant one.

> (1) *The ax is laid unto the root of the trees. Every
> tree therefore that bringeth not forth good fruit is
> hewn down, and cast into the fire* (Luke 3:9).

> (2) *If the salt has lost its savour,... it is thence-
> forth good for nothing, but to be cast out, and to
> be trodden under foot of men* (Mat. 5:13).

> (3) We risk rejection by God and enslavement by
> man. *If ye will not harken unto me, and will not
> do all these commandments;... I will set my face
> against you, and... they that hate you shall reign
> over you* (Lev. 26:14,17).

Is the Situation Hopeless? What God Promises

Abandonment Theologists would have us believe
that America's fall is irreversible. They claim that we are
living in the "end times," the "last days," that resistance

is futile. Some say the sooner we fall, the better. We will get to heaven that much sooner.

Such a position means surrendering our freedoms by default. This is in stark disobedience to the will and directives of God. Who authorized the clergy to put His return on *our* timetable rather than wait for *His?* The decision as to whether America collapses or undergoes a miraculous recovery is God's decision, not ours, and will be in response to our prayers and actions.

The Scriptures clearly reveal the evil, enslaving spiritual war that is waged relentlessly against us and how we can prevail and triumph over it. Christians are commanded to:

> *Put on the whole armour of God, that ye may be able to stand against the wiles of the devil. Above all, taking the shield of faith, wherewith ye shall be able to quench all the fiery darts of the wicked. And take the helmet of salvation, and the sword of the Spirit, which is the word of God: praying always....*(Eph. 6:11,16-18).

We are then to go and *teach all nations ... to observe all things whatsoever I have commanded you* (Mat. 28:19-20).

These are the works of faith, of loyalty and obedience to God that brought light in the darkness, that turned back the *fiery darts of the wicked* (Eph. 6:16) and produced America's liberty! This was the faith of the Fathers in action.

A person in this spiritual battle whose rationale and logic are Spiritually dead cannot even begin to comprehend the nature of the forces in conflict, let alone be a bulwark against evil. History evidences the fact that the secular world, lacking the Spiritual vision which comes through salvation and whose morality is based on situational ethics, is easy game to be enlisted into the cause of its own destruction.

God requires obedience. But He also rewards it. Listen to His promises, all applicable to America today:

(1) *When thou art in tribulation, and all these things are come upon thee, even in the latter days, if thou turn to the Lord thy God, and shalt be obedient unto his voice; (For the Lord thy God is a merciful God;) he will not forsake thee, neither destroy thee,...* (Deut. 4:30-31). God says that He ultimately determines our fate, not we. He has the power to intercede even at the last instant when all appears lost. Furthermore, God promises that He *will* intercede if we will turn back to Him and obey Him.

(2) *At what instant I shall speak concerning a nation, and concerning a kingdom, to pluck up, and to pull down, and to destroy it; If that nation, against whom I have pronounced, turn from their evil, I will repent of the evil that I thought to do unto them* (Jer. 18:7-8). Again God tells His people that it is He who determines the fate of nations. Hope is ever-present, and the potential to receive God's blessings is never extinguished. This same message of hope is given throughout the Scriptures. God never breaks His promises. *Draw nigh to God, and he will draw nigh to you* (Jas. 4:8).

(3) *If my people, which are called by my name, shall humble themselves, and pray, and seek my face, and turn from their wicked ways; then will I hear from heaven, and will forgive their sin, and will heal their land* (II Chron. 7:14). This is probably the most quoted of God's promises of hope to a nation. It totally negates any justification for an attitude of futility or surrender of one's freedoms by default. This is a promise from the Author of liberty Who sent His own Son to earth in the cause of liberty. God is ever-patient and merciful and withholds His final judg-

ment until the chance for a fallen nation's repentance has passed. He has given us examples: Ninevah was in decadence and moral collapse, certainly deserving of judgment. But the inspired Jonah electrified the people with the Word of God, who then turned back to God, Who healed their land.

(4) *When the enemy shall come in like a flood, the Spirit of the Lord shall lift up a standard against him* (Isa. 59:19). Again God is telling us that He is ever-present and in command, that even when the enemy comes in full force He has the power to stop him. And He will, as He proved throughout history, if we first meet His conditions.

(5) *But cleave unto the Lord your God, as ye have done unto this day. For the Lord hath driven out from before you great nations and strong: but as for you, no man hath been able to stand before you unto this day. One man of you shall chase a thousand: for the Lord your God, he it is that fighteth for you, as he hath promised you. Take good heed therefore unto yourselves, that ye love the Lord your God* (Josh. 23:8-11). This is what happened in the American Revolution. That little, underfunded, under-armed militia of George Washington's had God as its companion in the battles for a cause which glorified Christ and the Father. The powerful British did not prevail because the Continental Army prayed continuously and never forgot God. Today if America undergoes a Spiritual revival and turns back to God, we also will be able to proclaim that "one chased a thousand."

Our Real Responsibilities

Understanding these Biblical principles leads us to a handful of practical obligations. First, we must go to the

Lord in prayer, ask forgiveness and recommit ourselves personally and as a nation to obedience to Him.

Second, we must become learned enough in America's Christian and political history to understand that the 1947 Supreme Court's concept of a two-way wall of separation between church and state, which has neutralized and paralyzed the relationship between Christian citizens and our government, has no foundation in history or case law. The concept is a deadly threat to America's freedoms which were founded on the sacred duty of her Christian citizens to be certain their political leaders conduct government's affairs according to the civil and moral laws and codes of the Bible.

Third, we must understand that the Abandonment Clergy's "end times" and "last days" theories are what they are - speculations. In fact such speculations are dangerous at an hour when our children's future hangs by a thread, and boldness and greatness are required of committed Christians.

Almost everyone senses the desperation of the times as they witness an acceleration of wars and upheavals happening every day throughout the world. People sense that America is facing increasing danger. Some say, "Pity the children. I'm glad I've lived my life." How could a Christian citizen, whose life is committed to the service and cause of Christ, make such a statement of resignation and despair?

On the surface such a statement would seem to reflect the ultimate selfishness. But does it really? More likely it reflects the ultimate confusion. How could he or she justify sitting on the bleachers, impotently watching the disintegration of our nation's heritage, in view of the full-action charges from Christ? It isn't a matter of their ill will. If these same people knew what to do, many would sacrifice anything necessary in the noblest of all causes.

Only one answer can explain why so many well-meaning Christians are paralyzed into inaction: the Abandonment Clergy and their followers have been teaching, preaching and saturating the media and their church members with the doctrine of surrender and political non-involvement. They are not teaching us to surrender to Christ through obedience to the commandments of God. Rather, they tell us that America is finished, that the collapse of our heritage and our freedoms has been predetermined within a definable near-future time frame and is therefore beyond our control.

The legitimate study of eschatology (the future in prophecy) has been converted into a doctrine of futility and surrender by the clergy who, in defiance of Christ's injunction (See Mark 13:32,33), insist upon assigning near-future dates to the "last days," the "rapture of the church" and the "second coming" of Christ.

> *The Abandonment Clergy and their followers have been teaching, preaching and saturating the media and their church members with the doctrine of surrender and political non-involvement.*

Imagine the anguish and resentment our present-day youth will feel when they realize that their parents and grandparents abandoned the fight to save America under the banner of passive "love" and of the imminent "end times" and "last days." No doubt many of the "end-times" clergy do not understand the invincible power of faith over evil and are themselves caught up in the "America is lost" syndrome. But the clergy, as representatives of Christ, have a sacred duty to be learned in the Scriptures about issues so fundamental as whether a true Christian can retreat to the bleachers or must be on the battlefront in full hope and faith that God will grant victory to the faithful as He has so often done in history.

The Abandonment Clergy's congregations and followers must take them to task and demand that they stop
selling futility in the name of Christ. At the very least the
clergy should understand that their "last days" teachings
are nothing more than personal speculations. Christ
taught that futility of attitude denies the faith and leads
to enslavement. He promised great rewards for those
who endure to the end in His cause of freedom. (See Mat.
5:10,12... and many other references including Revelation).

In summary the Christian mandate is expressed in
many ways. No one who commits his life to Christ can
mistake His marching orders to the faithful:

- *Stand fast in the liberty wherewith Christ hath
  made us free* (Gal. 5:1);
- *Who will rise up for me against the workers of
  iniquity?* (Ps. 94:16);
- *Occupy till I come* (Luke 19:13);
- *Be strong in the Lord, and in the power of his
  might* (Eph. 6:10);
- *Put on the whole armour of God, that ye may be
  able to stand against the wiles of the devil* (Eph.
  6:11);
- *And take the helmet of salvation, and the sword
  of the Spirit, which is the word of God*
  (Eph. 6:17);
- *For God hath not given us the spirit of fear; but
  of power, and of love, and of a sound mind* (II
  Tim. 1:7);
- *The righteous are bold as a lion* (Prov. 28:1);
- *O Timothy, keep that which is committed to thy
  trust...* (I Tim. 6:20).

God is absolutely consistent throughout both Testaments in His call to action. He offers no hint of tolerance
for abandonment but rather provides many examples of
the consequences to such individuals and to nations.

This is the Christian's *call to greatness,* a call urgent in its need to be heard today. Futility, hopelessness, surrender by default, surrender by false interpretation of the "last days" and the "end times" have no place in the spirit or conduct of the people of God. Such surrender serves only one master - Satan - and leads a free nation to only one destiny - destruction. America is well on its way, not as a result of any irreversible tide of history as the Marxists would have us believe but *as a direct result of the inversion of basic doctrinal mandates to action.*

Deadly Inversions of the Christian Faith

Following is a summary of two of the deadliest inversions:

(1) LOVE: one of the most powerful terms in the Scriptures, the centerpiece of the mission of Christ, has been stripped of its very essence - obedience to the commandments which themselves represent a declaration of war on evil in all of its manifestations. The inverted meaning of "love" reduces the faith down to virtuous but non-controversial activities on the "reservation" and an interpretation of "love" as a passive sentimentalism. The teeth have thus been pulled from Satan's archenemy, leaving Christians defenseless in their ability for discernment of truth from error, good from evil, and wide open to the *wiles of the devil* (Eph.6:11) who is the "master of deceit."

(2) Over-application of a branch of theology known as eschatology, in which signs and evidences of the prophesied end times are used to date the "last days" as being in the very near future, thus creating often-heard attitudes of futility and despair: "Why bother? It's all but over anyway"; a misinterpretation of "We're in this world,

not of it"; "America is under God's judgment and is irreversibly going the way of ancient, pagan Rome"; "The 'rapture' and 'return of Christ' are imminent at any moment."

The clergy who preach these doctrines or doctrines which draw those conclusions are in reality preaching disobedience to the commandments of Christ and abdication of duty. *Fear God, and keep his commandments; for this is the whole duty of man* (Eccl. 12:13). In our surrender we give up our God-given American heritage without a fight.

The inversion trivializing the meaning of love and the inversion of the purpose of the legitimate, inspiring study of eschatology have proven to be two more of Satan's greatest triumphs as America's liberties vanish at an increasing rate.

In summary what has been happening to us as a nation? The obvious answer, in Biblical expression, is that America has been "forgetting God." What are the predictable consequences? *All nations that forget God... shall be turned into hell* (Ps. 9:17). The good news, however, is that America can stop her plunge into the New World Order with its godless One-World Government. The movement can be reversed by truly faithful, clear-minded Christians, including much of the clergy, who are made aware of these travesties perpetrated upon them by the master of deceit, Satan.

The Scriptures cry out, *Choose this day whom you will serve* (Josh. 24:15). Note the expression "serve." "Serve" is a full-action term, the ultimate expression of "works." It is the outpouring evidence of true faith and commitment to God. God makes no room in His army for pacifists or those who live by the futility and defection of Abandonment Theology.

Christ declares that there can be no "lukewarm" commitment (See Rev. 3:16) to His service, no compromise with evil and no shade of abandonment. There is no substitute for eternal vigilance.

How Do You Rate?

Based on the above, how do you rate yourself? Are you a "bleachers" Christian, watching your country disintegrate and your children's future succumb to a tidal wave of evil and darkness while you do nothing or halfheartedly do something? Or are you a committed warrior in the conquering army of Christ, giving your very best according to your calling?

CHAPTER EIGHT

WHAT WILL IT TAKE TO SAVE OUR COUNTRY?

Introduction

This book has shown that the freedoms which America has enjoyed were made possible for us by God through His Son Jesus Christ. These same freedoms were born at Calvary and nearly 2000 years later became the foundation of our great nation through the faith and sacrifices of the Founding Fathers, the colonial clergy and citizens during the struggle for independence.

America's invincible strength, her free enterprise economic system, the countless freedoms and blessings enjoyed by her individual citizens were all products and benefits of the Founding Fathers' love of and commitment to Jesus Christ. In fact so impassioned was their love of Christ and loyalty to Him that the battle cry of the Revolution was "No king but King Jesus!"

Today that passion and those treasures are being lost. Nearly everybody knows it and is experiencing it, but only a few understand what went wrong or what to do. The resulting vacuum is being filled by a satanic evil that is enslaving the mind of the American Christian and dragging it into the pit of confusion and increased vulnerability to Satan's deceits and lies. Soon, as things are going, America's citizens may themselves be reduced to political and physical bondage.

So ominous are the approaching, near-future consequences to our children that an increasingly common
expression among adults has become, "I'm glad I've lived
my life and don't have to face what today's poor kids are
facing. I wish there were something I could do."

It is possible that you will experience what "those
poor kids" are facing which may be nothing short of a hell
on earth much like the sufferings of multiplied millions
of men, women and children described in the chapter
"Military Vulnerability." The paramount question among
those who see it coming and have not yet succumbed to
the fatalism of the Abandonment Theologists is "Can
America be saved? If so, what can I do?"

I believe that America can be saved and again
brought to true greatness. But there is a reality that we
must first accept. The cause of America's sickness, that
which is bringing her to the doorstep of the death of her
freedoms, is fundamentally spiritual.

America's abandonment of God, the Author of her
liberties, is nothing new. It has been going on for decades.
Accordingly, no quick-fix remedy is going to save her.
People ask, "If there is no quick fix, what, precisely, will
it take to bring her back, to defeat our mortal enemies?"

The expected answer would be "Let's get back to the
Bible." But is that sufficient? What does it mean? If we
wish to take action, there must be an Action Guide, a
framework within which we as individuals can act with
maximum efficiency according to our "calling," an overall
framework in which every integral part makes sense in
terms of the total battle.

What is that framework called? In previous chapters
we called it the Christian or Biblical Worldview.

God Speaks to the Crucial Issues

There is no reason for Christians to be confused about anything that's going on in the world today or about the solutions. For example, in matters of civil law and government the Bible is clear. America's Constitution and Bill of Rights are founded upon God's civil laws. If their roots weren't in the Bible, the various articles and amendments would never have made it into the Constitution.

What about issues such as national defense? Their foundations are in the Bible, too. God describes in detail the "fallen nature" of man and his propensity, if left unchecked, to enslave his fellow man. The Book of Nehemiah leaves no question about the imperative for an invincible military defense capability if national freedom is to be maintained. This is nothing beyond the understanding of the average Christian today and is the responsibility of the clergy to teach it.

As described earlier in this book, even the very checks-and-balances structure of our government (executive, legislative, judicial) is rooted in the Bible specifically in the Book of Isaiah.

What about the Biblical Worldview and the UN? We constantly hear about the glories of the United Nations and a coming New World Order in which America would be under the authority of a UN-based world government. Her national independence and sovereignty would be lost, her citizens would be disarmed, and her ability to defend herself militarily would be non-existent. We would be protected by UN "peace forces." Why should we be concerned when the UN Charter speaks glowingly of human rights, and the whole objective of such a world government is that of "peace"? Who could possibly disagree with that professed intent? Is it realistic? Is it possible, considering some of the member nations and their treatment of their own citizens? Does God take a position? Should your clergyman take a position?

Yes, God does take a position, and He explains it in much detail. If the Abandonment Clergy truly taught the Biblical Worldview, there would be no question in the mind of any American Christian regarding God's mandate for our national sovereignty as a condition of freedom in this fallen world. Nor would there be any issue about the inevitable results of our Christian nation attempting to achieve "peace" with godless, atheistic nations whose bloody history speaks for itself.

Let's get to the ultimate truth on the subject of national defense and the policies that have brought us to the critical condition we face today from an increasing proliferation of deadly adversaries.

If the Abandonment Clergy truly taught the Biblical Worldview, there would be no question in the mind of any American Christian regarding God's mandate for our national sovereignty as a condition of freedom in this fallen world.

Should we have trusted the atheistic enemies of America, which we did through the 1972 ABM Treaty and a succession of other treaties known as SALT I, SALT II, START I and START II? Should that be a complex question for the average Christian? Should Christians have remained essentially mute when in 1961 they were informed of President Kennedy's presentation to the UN of the infamous U.S. State Dept. Document 7277 (discussed in Chapter Three)? It called for the three-stage disarmament of the United States and her citizens and the subordination of our sovereignty to a World Government enforced by the godless United Nations. What would George Washington, Thomas Jefferson, James Madison, John Adams, John Quincy Adams and John Jay have said - unanimously?

And what would the colonial clergy and the average colonists have said - unanimously? That requires no speculation. Having been schooled since their earliest childhood in the Bible, they would have referred to the Bible as their ultimate authority and declared that for America to engage in such folly could only result in the death of her freedoms and the enslavement of her people. They would be astounded that it could have happened in our time without a Christian revolt in response.

But it did because the Christians of our generation have lost their Christian Worldview through its mutilation and distortion by the Abandonment Clergy.

What Can I Do?

In view of the above, let's consider some answers to the crucial question, "What can I do?" asked by Christians who realize that things are desperately wrong and that the lamp of America's liberties is possibly close to being suddenly extinguished.

Requirement #1: PASSION
It is likely that America's Christians today will have to match the passion of the Founding Fathers, who concluded the Declaration of Independence, "...we mutually pledge to each other our lives, our fortunes, and our sacred honor." Their commitment reflected the passion of the clergy and the citizens, and it must be revived today in America.

To dramatize the point, it's worth telling a story about Aristotle and a young man.

"Sir, How Can I Become Like You?"

A young boy was a fervent admirer of the great philosopher, Aristotle. One day he approached Aristotle and asked, "Sir, how can I become like you?"

"Come with me," Aristotle beckoned the boy. He took him to the shore of a great body of water and walked out until the boy was waist deep. Suddenly, Aristotle grabbed the boy by the back of his neck and thrust his head under the water. At first the surprised boy did nothing. But soon he began to run out of breath and tried to stand up. Aristotle held him under. His heart pounding and lungs about to burst, the boy panicked and began to thrash frantically as he sought to free himself from Aristotle's death grip. At the last instant Aristotle pulled the boy's head out of the water. With a great gasp the boy filled his lungs with a rush of life-giving air.

"Son," remarked Aristotle, "when you desire to gain knowledge with the same passion that you desired that air, then you can become like me."

The obvious parallel is that God demands the same passion, desire and resolve from all of us if we truly wish to regain the blessings of His liberty and save our country. No "lukewarm," compromising commitment will work. The only way is to be "hot" (See Rev. 3:16). We must commit ourselves to His cause of spiritual and political liberty (cause and effect) with ...*all* [our] *heart, with all* [our] *soul, and with all* [our] *mind* (Mat. 22:37). That is, with total commitment. That's why that verse is known as the *first and great commandment* (Mat. 22:38).

What about our emotions? Is it a sin to be angry about what has happened to us? Absolutely not. Any person who realizes and understands the horrible things that have transpired in recent years and their pending consequences should be angry, perhaps outright enraged, about the betrayal of America's security by the political leaders we trusted. The challenge now is to turn that righteous indignation, that fury, into positive, constructive action.

Requirement #2: PRAYER

Our prayers cannot be passive. They must be filled with passion of the same intensity described above. If the light of truth and reality has suddenly turned on for you and you truly desire to do something meaningful for our country and for your loved ones, God wants you to pray with passion and intensity as you ask Him to reveal His truth and mission for you:

> *The effectual fervent prayer of a righteous man availeth much* (Jas. 5:16).

That kind of prayer was the fountainhead of the faith of the Fathers that brought forth miracles from an intervening God against otherwise impossible odds. God promises, as earlier shown in this book, that those miracles can be repeated in our time. Accordingly, there is no justification for despair.

Our first task is to go to our knees in prayer and ask God to help us put the shattered pieces of our Christian Worldview back together so we can clearly see the whole picture and the positive role that we as individuals can play in the areas of our calling. Then get on with the necessary aggressive action on the battlefronts.

Freedom's Actions

Bearing in mind that there is no quick fix for America's ills:

(1) Get your prayer life in order. Always pray with an open Bible and ask God to reveal His will for you. Prayer brings revelation and power.

(2) Read the Bible from cover to cover. Your worldview will come together because God is absolutely consistent from generation to generation. *The word of the Lord endureth to all generations* (Ps. 100:5; I Pet. 1:25). Issues and events will change, but never God's laws of freedom and righteousness, never His definition of the deceitful, deadly nature of the enemies of freedom, never His directives about confronting evil and defeating it in all of its manifestations with full faith that He will help us. By reading and studying the Bible, you will understand the times and know what to do (See I Chron. 12:32).

(3) Never trust the obvious. We live in a time of unprecedented deception, and Satan is a master of deceit. Reference every important issue to the Word and truth of God. He speaks to all issues. *There is a way that seems right to a man, but its end is the way of death* (Prov. 14:12).

(4) Be a family person. Be loyal to your mate and a great parent to your children. The family institution was established by God, and it is the centerpiece of America's freedoms.

(5) Read books on the great political issues. Learn to think Biblically about political issues. The Bible is the greatest book ever written on politics. Our American Constitutional Republic and free enterprise system are structured upon its civil laws and moral codes beginning with the Ten Commandments. Politics and the Christian "religion" are inseparable. Never talk politics and religion? Except in the most superficial ways, that's a near impossibility for one who is intellectually honest.

(6) Be politically active. Register to vote and work to elect God-fearing righteous men and women to office. This is a Biblical mandate to every responsible Christian citizen in return for his freedoms. Research your political candidates' backgrounds and public statements. The organizations in Appendix B will give you biographies and voting records on political candidates.

(7) Read this book again. It will greatly expand your Biblical Worldview and help you in your witness.

(8) Sponsor Creation seminars in your church. It is vital that your fellow Christians understand Creation as a science in order to dispute the claims of evolutionists. Organizations in Appendix B can point you to the best seminars.

(9) Sponsor American Heritage seminars in your church. Unless Christians understand the significance of America's founding and history, they cannot comprehend the magnitude of how far we have strayed from our Founding Fathers' work. Organizations in Appendix B can point you to the best ones.

(10) Find a potential leader among young people and sponsor him or her to a Christian, conservative leadership school such as Summit Ministries which first grounds its students in a solid Christian Worldview (See Appendix B).

(11) Subscribe to leading-edge Christian, conservative news journals such as the "Summit Journal" and others published by the front-line organizations listed in Appendix B.

(12) Take a firm stand on at least one major moral issue such as abortion, homosexuality, school prayer, etc., research it, and let your stand be known.

(13) Publish your positions in the Op-Ed columns and Letters to the Editor columns of your newspaper, and call "talk radio" shows and voice your opinions. One such article and/or one call could reach hundreds of thousands of people. Go to the library and research how to write your letters with maximum effectiveness. And be confident in vocalizing your views. Be relentless. Our enemies are!

(14) Contact the battlefront organizations listed in Appendix B and get on their mailing lists - all of them. Study the volumes of priceless, researched information they will send you. This will educate you and keep you informed about a vast number of political issues and what the Bible says about them. Step-by-step, your Christian Worldview will come together. Remember, God is consistent throughout the Testaments. Once intact, your Worldview will effectively be anchored. Issues and circumstances will change but not God's laws of freedom. Be aggressive!

(15) Make yourself heard by your political representatives about critical issues such as defense. Follow up and require answers. Use the telephone, registered letter, fax, make a personal visit, telegram. Turn on the heat. You're the boss. Your government representatives are your employees. If necessary, demand that they respond, *not* with patronizing answers but with facts. Ask why they are allowing America to militarily disarm and to be defenseless against attacking ICBMs. Contact the pro-defense organizations in Appendix B and let them arm you with the real facts.

Political action is a product of knowledge. This Action Guide is showing you how to acquire that knowledge from some of the best sources.

(16) Run for School Board and keep the textbook selection honest. If evolution is taught, insist that the Creationist position be taught as a scientific counterbalance. Contact the Institute for Creation Research (see Appendix B), an organization of elite, credentialed scientists in all of the disciplines. They will show you the most effective political process and equip you with the necessary materials.

(17) Confront your clergyman if you determine that he is selling Abandonment Theology. Give him a copy of this book and ask for answers. You will find that many Abandonment Theology clergymen are themselves victims either of their seminaries or through the books and writings of other theologians, and some will admit it. When the manuscript of this book was broadcast nationwide on the radio, many appreciative clergymen called. Your clergyman's true intentions will quickly become clear.

   If your clergyman is already "in our camp," thank him for his stands and give him a copy of this book. He may find it useful in his witness to others and as a sourcebook for them.

(18) Always do what is right, and trust God for the result. Jesus never compromised or bargained with evil. He came to destroy it, and He gave *us* the power to be victorious over it. Confront evil and win! But if you try to compromise or coexist with it, like a cancer, evil will overtake and destroy you.

Conclusion

   All of the above actions and suggestions have the overall objective of guiding you to a firm, well-defined Christian Worldview from which God's will and directives for you as a warrior in His cause will become obvious or easily discovered.

It is essential that we understand that most wars in history and those today are essentially clashes between opposing worldviews. Of those threatening America today, the Marxist/Leninist and secular humanist worldviews are most critical.

The Marxist/Leninist worldview is totally anathema to the Christian Worldview. The Marxist assigns no value to human life except in its relation to the state. His process for achieving utopia among men includes "ethnic cleansing," mass killings, genocide and a socialist state. Marxism/Leninism is the archenemy of Jesus Christ. It offers slavery, misery and death. Christ offers freedom, happiness and life.

> *When your heart becomes filled with the love of Christ, and you have committed your life to His service, He will give you vision and understanding through His Word, the Bible.*

Secular humanism, another deadly worldview, has long dominated our public schools. Its doctrines are also irreconcilable with the Christian Worldview which is why God was outlawed in the classrooms. Secular humanism is the fertile ground of evolution which denies a personal, loving, interventional, freedom-authoring God. Secular humanism disputes the absolute, eternal laws of morality and liberty and places no limits upon fallen man's propensity toward enslavement of his fellow man. Given the pervasiveness of secular humanism in our schools, is it any wonder that catastrophe has afflicted the lives of such vast numbers of America's young people, her future leaders?

The Christians of America, having let their traditional Worldview become corrupted, shattered and compromised by the Abandonment Clergy, have been unable to cope with the invading secular humanist worldview.

Had the Founding Fathers been secular humanists, there would have been no Declaration of Independence, no Constitution, no Bill of Rights, no God-given "unalienable right" of the individual to life, liberty and the pursuit of happiness.

Yet it is we who still have at our disposal the superior, available power and strength to "take it all back." The hour is late, but the bell has not yet tolled for America. There is still a choice. You can still become part of a reborn "standard." *When the enemy shall come in like a flood, the Spirit of the Lord shall lift up a standard against him* (Isa. 59:19).

If you choose to heed God's calling and engage in the battle for America, all of your life will become enriched - your marriage, your relationship with your children, your excellence in your profession. The light and truth of God will expose and vaporize the deceit, error, confusion and evil of Satan who never rests, who relentlessly attacks you on every front, who has come *to steal, and to kill, and to destroy* (John 10:10).

Your Christian Worldview will enable you to *Put on the whole armour of God* (Eph. 6:11), *take the sword of the Spirit, which is the word of God* (Eph. 6:17) and, through the power of the Holy Spirit, triumph over Satan regardless of the apparent odds. *One man of you shall chase a thousand: for the Lord your God, he it is that fighteth for you, as he hath promised you.* (Josh. 23:10).

When your heart becomes filled with the love of Christ and you have committed your life to His service, He will give you vision, understanding and power through His Word, the Bible. You will become free from the bondage of Satan. God will give you an inner happiness and power through a life of direction, purpose and fulfillment. Your example will become a witness and an inspiration to others because your Christian Worldview will position you on the cutting edge of the action in both personal and political life.

A rebirth of the Christian Worldview of the Fathers is what it will take to save America and our children from the horrors we are facing. Today we are swamped in an increasing tidal wave of evil on every front which has found its access through the worldviews of secular humanism and Marxism/Leninism which have increasingly dominated our public educational systems and public institutions to the exclusion of God.

> *Had the Fathers been secular humanists, there would have been no Declaration of Independence, no Constitution, no Bill of Rights, no God-given "unalienable right" of the individual to life, liberty, and the pursuit of happiness.*

Whose business is this? According to the Bible, it is your business, my business, the church's business.

For America to survive, and triumph, her Christian citizens have no alternative but to engage in the struggles on every front. But there is an old truism, "Action without knowledge breeds chaos and confusion." This book is an Action Guide designed to show you the way to gain that knowledge.

In Joel 3:9 God calls forth *the mighty men* and even the weak: *Let the weak say, I am strong* (Joel 3:9,10). Remember how much power is available to Christians today! *I give you power to tread on serpents ... and over all the power of the enemy* (Luke 10:19). That same call goes out to us today.

There is no short cut, no quick fix. What is required is hard, diligent, courageous work. Satan has taken America to the edge, and we can rest assured that he will spare no effort in going for the final kill. No aspect of personal or national life has escaped him.

As our abortion mills slaughter the innocent by the millions, homosexuality (which God terms "abomination") enjoys free reign, our government, by intent, disarms our military defenses in an increasingly dangerous world and America collapses in her Biblical morality, God's call to every citizen, in particular to every Christian, could not be more clear.

America is in great need of help and commitment from her citizens - from you and me. How much commitment do we need?

Reflecting back to America's founding, how much passion and commitment were required in bringing forth our country? How much did Patrick Henry have? His thunderous "Give me liberty, or give me death!" resonated with his commitment. We have heard many stories about the sufferings of the Founding Fathers during the Revolutionary War: death by torture, wealthy men dying in poverty having committed their entire fortunes to the war effort, families killed and Founders dying of heartbreak.

But what about the passion of the Father of our country, George Washington? On June 12, 1776 Washington wrote a letter to his cousin Lund in which he expressed his recognition of the seeming impossibility for victory. Did Washington give up, as many of today's bleachers Christians are doing in response to their Abandonment Clergy? Here, in part, is how he bared his heart.

> I wear a countenance dressed in a calm serenity of perfect confidence, while my heart is corroded with infinite apprehension. ...I'm not afraid to die. Why should I? I am afraid to die only with infamy and disgrace. Heaven knows how truly I love my country, that I embark on this arduous enterprise on the purest motives... If it be the will of God that America should be independent

of Great Britain...even I and those...men...may not be thought unworthy instruments in His hands. In this persuasion I resolve to go on, contented to save my country or die in the last ditch.[121]

This is an example of the courage that Christ requires of us, the courage which gave us the Godly heritage we have long enjoyed but have neglected even in clear view of the relentless attacks against it. Washington went to God, and then he went to battle.

Are we prepared to go to the limit, as did Washington, the Fathers and much of the citizenry, to head off and turn back the obvious fate that awaits us and our children if we do *not* act?

A Concluding Prayer

The words from one of our nation's most loved songs, *America:*

My country, 'tis of Thee, Sweet land of liberty, Of thee I sing: Land where my fathers died, Land of the pilgrims' pride, From every mountain side Let freedom ring!

Our fathers' God, to Thee, Author of liberty, to Thee we sing: Long may our land be bright With freedom's holy light; Protect us by Thy might, Great God, our King!

"One Indissoluble Bond"

The highest glory of the American Revolution was this; it connected in one indissoluble bond the principles of civil government with the principles of Christianity.
- John Quincy Adams, July 4th, 1821[122]

Americans combine the notions of Christianity and of liberty so intimately in their minds, that it is impossible to make them conceive of one without the other.
-Alexis deTocqueville[123]

APPENDIX A - PART ONE

THE PERSON OF CHRIST

In order for us to fully appreciate the priceless heritage handed down to us by America's Founding Fathers and the Source of the power of their faith, it is necessary to understand the central figure in the faith of the Fathers from which they derived their wisdom, vision and power. Let us, therefore, focus on Jesus Christ Himself and His complete uniqueness. He is available to us today through His Holy Spirit, just as He was to the Fathers.

Could America Have Been Founded by Another Religion ?

Today it is widely taught that "All religions are basically the same," that their prophets teach the same basic moral and legal codes. But, are they the same? Except for similar moral codes, can any "religion" be equated to Christianity?

If so, why haven't other religions produced declarations of independence and constitutions that exalt and protect the individual, declare that he is created in the image of God and has a Divine right to be free, made the tyrant tremble and rendered national military invincibility as did the Christian faith of the Founding Fathers?

What's the difference? Why and how does Christianity liberate men from the bondage of sin, corruption and political tyranny while by historical and contemporary contrast other religions tend to subordinate the individual to harsh systems of freedom-denying legalism, or worse? The following commentary addresses these questions and was excerpted through item (7) from *Many Infallible Proofs*, by Henry M. Morris.

The difference lies in the *person* of Christ. Biblical Christianity is absolutely unique in the nature of its central personage and founder, Jesus Christ. There is none other like Him in all of history or even in all literature. Some writers, of course, presume to place Christ as merely one in a list of great religious leaders, but this is absurd. He stands in contrast to all others, not in line with them, not even at the head of the line. His uniqueness is illustrated in the following partial list of His attributes:

(1) Anticipation of His coming. His coming was prophesied in fine detail as to lineage, birthplace, time, career, purpose, nature of death, resurrection, etc., hundreds of years prior to His actual appearance. There has never been any other religious leader - indeed, no other man - in all of history for which this was true.

(2) The Virgin Birth. Christ's virgin birth stands entirely alone; nothing like it was ever imagined elsewhere. God Himself took up residence in a virgin's womb, thence to be born in a fully natural human birth with no actual genetic connection to human parents.

(3) The Divine Human Nature. Although there have been power-crazed dictators and fanatics who have claimed to be God, even these individuals recognized and acknowledged that their assumption of divinity was only relative - they hardly imagined that they had created the stars or even their own mothers! But Jesus Christ was

God in the highest sense, the Creator of all things (See Col. 1:16), and He claimed to be God on many occasions and in many ways. He was also man in the fullest sense except that He had no sin. He was not half man and half God but rather all man and all God in a perfect and indissoluble union. No other man was ever thus - indeed, no other man ever claimed to be thus.

(4) Sinless. Of no one else in history could the claim ever be made in seriousness that he lived a whole lifetime without one sin, in thought or word or deed. But this very thing was claimed by Jesus' closest friends, by His worst enemies, by the greatest of the apostles and by Jesus, Himself. Peter said, *He did no sin* (I Peter 2:22), and John said, *In him is no sin* (I John 3:5). Judas said, *I have betrayed the innocent blood* (Mat. 27:4), and Pilot said, *I find in him no fault at all* (John 18:38).

(5) Unique Teachings. The Sermon on the Mount is without parallel. The beauty and power of the Upper Room discourse, the compelling majesty of the Sermon on the Mount of Olives, the power of His parables, and all His other teachings are separated by a great gulf from even the finest teachings of other men. And yet His teachings continually include both the claim and the internal awareness that He was uniquely God's Son. In no other religious writings does one find such a phenomenon as this.

(6) His Unique Death. He said, *It is finished, and he bowed his head, and gave up the ghost* (John 19:30). Literally, He "dismissed His Spirit." It is evidently quite a difficult task even to commit suicide, but certainly no one can simply decide to die and then, by his mere volition, proceed to die. But Jesus did! He said, *No man taketh it from me, but I lay it down of myself* (John 10: 18).

(7) His Resurrection. Other religions of the world (including Islam, Buddhism, Hinduism, Confucianism, Animism, Shintoism, Taoism, etc.) were founded by men who were, unlike Christ, sinful men. These founders are all in their graves, defeated by man's last enemy. Christ alone rose from the grave and defeated death.[124]

What was it that so bound the Fathers, the clergy and the colonists together that they were empowered to function as a great, unified body in the common cause of liberty? It was the Spirit of the living, personal, eternal, omnipresent, omnipotent, loving, resurrected Christ. The Founders did not have to reach up to some impersonal God and try to please Him through their good works and through their obedience to a mass of brutalizing laws enforced by the tyranny of man.

Christ declared that He was and is God; *I and my Father are one* (John 10:30), that He came personally to earth to dwell among us and teach us the way to personal salvation, to Spiritual and political freedom, to life in all of its dimensions. He taught that God is our loving, caring Father, that He is accessible through prayer and will answer our prayers. Christ brought the relationship between man and God out of the abstract into one that is intimate, personal and alive.

That's what we say about Him. But what did Christ say about Himself, directly and through His inspired apostles?

First let us distinguish Him from all other deities. Christ was part of the Trinity (One God in three Persons):

For there are three that bear record in heaven, the Father, the Word [the Son]*, and the Holy Ghost:*[the Holy Spirit] *and these three are one* (I John 5:7).

What is the Trinity? The concept that three equals one has long confused many Christians. There are several illustrations that help people cross that barrier: is such an abstract concept even possible? First use mathematics: instead of thinking 1+1+1, which clearly equals 3, ask how much is 1 x 1 x 1? Obviously, 1.

The Bible declares that things which cannot be seen can often be understood through nature. In fact, nature and our universe including our very existence, are structured as trinities.

Consider, for example,

(1) Past, present, future: Take away any element. What is left?

(2) Space, mass, time: Take away any element. What is left?

(3) Length, width, breadth: Take away any element. What is left?

Examples from nature are innumerable. Consider Father, Son, Holy Spirit. Suddenly the concept of a Triune Creator, one God in three persons, has entered the realm of feasibility because the principle of three-in-one is incontestably evident in nature. In fact with such evidence it could be argued that a triune God is more logical than a single God who created everything apart from His own nature, including man.

Who Is Jesus?

What did Jesus declare about Himself directly and through the prophets?

John 3:16   *For God so loved the world, that he gave his only begotten Son, that whosoever believeth in him should not perish, but have everlasting life.*

Rev. 1:8   *I am the Alpha and Omega, the
                beginning and the ending, saith the Lord,
                which is, and which was, and which is to
                come, the Almighty.*

John 1:1   *In the beginning was the Word, and the
                Word was with God, and the Word was
                God.* He (the Word) existed in the
                beginning with, and as, God.

John 1:3   *All things were made by him; and without
                him was not anything made that was made.*
                The Creator.

John 1:4   *In him was life; and the life was the light
                of men.* The Source of life and light.

John 1:10   *The world was made by him.*

John 1:14   *And the Word was made flesh, and dwelt
                among us...* Christ was God incarnate (part
                of the Trinity).

John 1:14   *...(and we beheld his glory, the glory as of
                the only begotten of the Father,) full of grace
                and truth.*

John 14:6   *I am the way,...* Christ is not assuming the
                role of a prophet and saying that "God" is
                the way. He Himself claimed to be the way.

John 14:6   *I am the truth...* He declared Himself to be
                the truth.

John 14:6   *I am the life....:* He declared Himself to be the
                life.

I John 5:11   *And this is the record, that God hath given to us eternal life, and this life is in his Son. He that hath the Son hath life;* He declared Himself to be the Source of eternal life.

Ps. 119:142   *Thy law is the truth...* He declared Himself to be the Law.

John 17:17   *Thy Word is truth...* He declared Himself to be the Word.

Ps. 119:151   *Thy commandments are truth.* He declared Himself to be the commandments.

John 15:1   *I am the true vine, and my Father is the husbandman.* He declared Himself to be the vine, the Father (God), the pruning caretaker.

John 15:5   *I am the vine, ye are the branches...* He declared His Divine relationship to man.

John 11:25   *I am the resurrection, and the life:...*

John 11:25-6   *He that believeth in me, though he were dead, yet shall he live:... And whosoever liveth and believeth in me shall never die:* He declared Himself to be the Source of eternal life.

Col. 2:2,3   *...Christ; in whom are hid all the treasures of wisdom and knowledge:* He declared Himself to contain all knowledge and wisdom.

Rom. 3:23-4   *All have sinned, and come short of the glory of God; Being justified freely by his grace through the redemption that is in Christ Jesus.* He declared that He has the power of redemption (to buy back for a price) and of justification (sinners absolved from sin).

Mat. 28:18   *All power is given unto me in heaven and in earth.* He declared that His power is total.

Mat. 9:6   *The Son of man hath power on earth to forgive sins.* He declared, as only God can, to have the power to forgive sins.

John 8:12   *I am the light of the world: he that followeth me shall not walk in darkness, but shall have the light of life.* He declared Himself to be light (truth).

II Cor. 3:17 *Where the Spirit of the Lord is, there is liberty.* He declared Himself to be the Author of liberty.

Gal. 5:1   *Stand fast therefore in the liberty wherewith Christ hath made us free, and be not entangled again with the yoke of bondage.* Again, Christ declared Himself to be the Author of liberty. It is argued, correctly, that this verse refers to Spiritual liberty from the bondage of sin and corruption. But in the wake of Spiritual liberty comes the revelation and power of truth, the mortal enemy of political tyranny. Irresistibly, when truth gains its foothold, political freedom results.

John 8:32   *Ye shall know the truth, and the truth shall make you free.* Christ is truth.

Conclusion

Who was the real founder of America? Was it an assemblage of the Fathers, the clergy and the colonists? Was it an "expositor" of the Scriptures such as John Calvin, whose revolutionary insights crystallized into many of the freedoms we know today? Or was it Martin Luther, who broke the papal tyranny and began the Protestant Reformation. Perhaps it was the Reverend John Wycliffe who in 1382 helped bring the Dark Ages to a conclusion by translating the Bible from Latin into English for the common man and discovered in the Scriptures the principle of government "of the people, by the people, and for the people."

In spite of their vast contributions that culminated in America's freedoms, none of these men ever claimed any role other than that of "expositor" or "translator" of the Bible. We can therefore draw no other conclusion than that Jesus Christ, beginning with the triumph of His resurrection, was the real Author of America's freedoms - the true Founder of America.

Clearly, Christ was the bedrock and centerpiece of the living, power-filled (Spirit-filled) faith of the Fathers, the colonists and their clergy that brought forth our Declaration of Independence and our American Constitutional Republic.

The Spiritual War - Opposite Objectives - Founding America

Whereas Satan came ... *to steal, and to kill, and to destroy* (John 10:10), the mission of Christ was the opposite:

For this purpose the Son of God was manifested,
that he might destroy the works of the devil (I
John 3:8).

He hath anointed me to... preach deliverance to
the captives... to set at liberty them that are
bruised (Luke 4:18).

Only God can conquer Satan. Only Christ, His Son,
can destroy the works of the devil and through His Holy
Spirit empower believers, born-again Christians, to do
the same. No prophet has such supernatural power. Thus
from the "fall of man" until the advent of Christ, the world
groaned on in Satan's enslavement and misery. But the
spirit of Satan's darkness and tyranny is no match for the
Spirit of Christ's light and liberty. *I am the light of the*
world: he that followeth me shall not walk in darkness,
but shall have the light of life (John 8:12).

The record of history speaks loudly that wherever
the roots of freedom have gone down anywhere in the
world there was One, and none other, Who went before.
Dr. D. James Kennedy powerfully encapsulates this fact
in his book *What If Jesus Had Never Been Born?*

More than a century ago, James Russell Lowell,
the great literary man who was a Minister of
State for the United States to England, was once
at a banquet where the Christian religion (the
mission enterprise, in particular) was being
attacked by scoffers. He spoke up and said, "I
challenge any skeptic to find a ten square mile
spot on this planet where they can live their
lives in peace and safety and decency, where
womanhood is honored, where infancy and old
age are revered, where they can educate their
children, where the Gospel of Jesus Christ has
not gone first to prepare the way. If they find

such a place, then I would encourage them to emigrate thither and there proclaim their unbelief."[125]

Truly, America could have been founded on no religion other than Christianity.

Our Mission

Abandonment Theology, and our task today:

Jesus set the example for all who claim to be His. Our task is to take up the cross (See Mat. 16:24) and carry on with His work. The urgency for commitment could not be greater because the cross is being increasingly abandoned in America. We are losing our God-given liberties as a floodtide of evil fills the void.

The good news is that Christ is still calling. He is still standing at the door (See Rev. 3:20), alive, present, willing to accept and empower all who believe and who ask Him in. It is not too late. This is the heritage of America; that is our Divine charge to pass down to our children. Are we up to the task?

APPENDIX A - PART TWO

THE CHRISTIAN IN ACTION

VERSES FOR MEMORY
The Mission of Christ
The Power of a Christian
Love, Faith and Works
Action, Duties of a Christian
Deadly Nature of the Enemy
Hope - The Promises of God
Mission of a Christian

It is essential in these times of confusion and national peril that Christians be able to demonstrate effectively to others their understanding of the times (See I Chron. 12:32), what the struggles are all about, the deceptions of Satan, why there is hope for America and what positive actions God expects from each of us who is called by His name.

The following Bible verses under their defining subtitles will enable you to develop a sharp, persuasive, highly effective witness by which you may help and inspire others in the areas of their concerns and needs.

These treasures, many of which are referenced to their applications in this book, are among the most powerful, focused and easily understood of God's truths as they span both Testaments and the centuries. Bear in mind that only circumstances and settings change, but *his truth endureth to all generations* (Ps. 100:5), p. 177.

You are urged to look up these references in the King James Version and commit them to memory so you will *...be ready always to give an answer to every man that asketh you a reason of the hope that is in you...* (I Peter 3:15).

The Mission of Christ

For God so loved the world, that he gave his only begotten Son, that whosoever believeth in him should not perish, but have everlasting life (John 3:16).

For by grace are ye saved through faith; and that not of yourselves: it is the gift of God: Not of works, lest any man should boast. For we are his workmanship, created in Christ Jesus unto good works, which God hath before ordained that we should walk in them (Eph. 2:8,9,10), pp. 123, 124, 131, 158.

(Christ's mission statement) [He] *hath anointed me to preach the gospel to the poor;...to preach deliverance to the captives, and the recovering of sight to the blind, to set at liberty them that are oppressed* (Luke 4:18), pp. 31, 115, 122, 129, 133.

The Son of God was manifested that he might destroy the works of the devil (I John 3:8), pp. 9, 29, 115, 122, 129, 133.

Where the Spirit of the Lord is, there is liberty (II Cor. 3:17), p. 104.

America was founded upon Jesus Christ and the Bible, ("the faith of the Fathers"), His teaching about man's fallen nature and of the blessings of obedience to God. This established our Constitution's "checks-and-

balances" structure known as the "separation of powers."
Isa. 33:22: *For the Lord is our judge* (establishing the
judiciary); *the Lord is our lawgiver* (establishing the
legislature); *the Lord is our king* (establishing the executive), p. 23.

The Power of a Christian

*I give you power to tread on serpents...and over all the
power of the enemy* (Luke 10:19), pp. 10, 129, 183.

*Submit yourselves therefore to God. Resist the devil, and
he will flee from you* (Jas. 4:7).

Greater is he that is in you, than he that is in the world (1
John 4:4), p. 125.

*And take the helmet of salvation, and the sword of the
Spirit, which is the word of God:* (Eph. 6:17), pp. 157, 182.

*I am the light of the world: he that followeth me shall not
walk in darkness, but shall have the light of life* (John
8:12), p. 114.

Love, Faith and Works

This is love, that we walk after his commandments (II
John 6), p. 120.

(WARNING) *He that saith, I know him, and keepeth not
his commandments, is a liar, and the truth* [Christ-ed] *is
not in him* (I John 2:4), p. 131.

(WARNING) *Whosoever doeth not righteousness is not of
God* (I John 3:10), p. 127.

(WARNING) *But wilt thou know, O vain man, that faith without works is dead?* (Jas. 2:20), p. 122, 126, 134.

(TOTAL COMMITMENT) *Thou shalt love the Lord thy God with all thy heart, and with all thy soul, and with all thy mind* (Mat. 22:37) *...called the first and great commandment* (Mat. 22:38), p. 11, 124, 159, 175.

Action, Duties of a Christian (Until Christ Returns)

Occupy till I come (Luke 19:13), pp. 10, 136, 147, 157, 166.

Fear God, and keep his commandments; for this is the whole duty of man (Eccl. 12:13), pp. 5, 12, 132, 158, 168.

The righteous are bold as a lion (Prov. 28:1), pp. 136, 157, 166.

The effectual fervent prayer of a righteous man availeth much (Jas. 5:16), p. 176.

Call unto me, and I will answer thee, and show thee great and mighty things, which thou knowest not (Jer. 33:3), p. 125.

Who will stand up for me against the workers of iniquity? (Ps. 94:16), pp. 119, 136, 157, 166.

Stand fast in the liberty wherewith Christ hath made us free (Gal. 5:1), pp. 119, 157, 166, 194.

Ye are the salt of the earth... Ye are the light of the world... Let your light so shine before men, that they may see your good works, and glorify your Father which is in heaven (Mat. 5:13-14,16), pp. 124, 136, 159, 160.

Be strong in the Lord, and in the power of his might (Eph. 6:10), p. 166.

And be not conformed to this world, but be ye transformed by the renewing of your mind,... (Rom. 12:2), pp. 125, 130.

Preach the word; be instant in season, and out of season; reprove, rebuke, exhort with all longsuffering and doctrine (II Tim. 4:1-2), p. 157.

For God hath not given us the spirit of fear; but of power, and of love, and of a sound mind (II Tim. 1:7), p. 166.

And take the helmet of salvation, and the sword of the Spirit, which is the word of God (Eph. 6:17), pp. 157, 161, 166.

O Timothy, keep that which is committed to thy trust... (I Tim. 6:20), pp. 158, 166.

Then said Jesus unto His disciples, *If any man will come after me, let him deny himself, and take up his cross, and follow me* (Mat. 16:24), p. 133.

If thou wilt enter into life, keep the commandments (Mat. 19:17), p. 158.

I know thy works, that thou are neither cold not hot: I would thou wert cold or hot. So then because thou art lukewarm, and neither cold nor hot, I will spue thee out of my mouth (Rev. 3:15, 16), pp. 115, 122, 127, 128, 175.

I command thee this day to love the Lord thy God, to walk in his ways, and to keep his commandments and his statutes and his judgments, that thou mayest live and multiply: and the Lord thy God shall bless thee in the land...(Deut. 30:16), p. 168.

Deadly Nature of the Enemy

For we wrestle not against flesh and blood, but against principalities, against powers, against the rulers of the darkness of this world, against spiritual wickedness in high places (Eph. 6:12), pp. 104, 126.

The thief [Satan-ed] *cometh not, but to steal, and to kill, and to destroy* (John 10:10), pp. 115, 141, 153, 158, 182, 195.

Their feet are swift to shed blood: destruction and misery are in their ways: And the way of peace they have not known: There is no fear of God before their eyes (Rom. 3:15-18), p. 115.

For out of the heart proceed evil thoughts, murderers, adulterers, fornicators, thefts, false witness, blasphemies: (Mat. 15:19).

The heart [of fallen man-ed] *is deceitful above all things, and desperately wicked:..*(Jer. 17:9), pp. 16, 103.

...your adversary the devil, as a roaring lion, walketh about, seeking whom he may devour:... (I Peter 5:8), p. 158.

Their throat is an open sepulchre; with their tongues they have used deceit;... (Rom 3:13).

Hope - The Promises of God

Draw nigh to God, and he will draw nigh to you (Jas. 4:8), pp. 11, 106.

If my people, which are called by my name, shall humble themselves, and pray, and seek my face, and turn from their wicked ways; then will I hear from heaven, and will forgive their sin, and will heal their land (II Chron. 7:14), p. 162.

When the enemy shall come in like a flood, the Spirit of the Lord shall lift up a standard against him (Isa. 59:19), pp. 163, 182.

One man of you shall chase a thousand: for the Lord your God, he it is that fighteth for you, as he hath promised you (Josh. 23:10), pp. 163, 182.

Mission of a Christian (The Great Commission)

Go ye therefore, and teach all nations, baptizing them in the name of the Father, and of the Son, and of the Holy Ghost: Teaching them to observe all things whatsoever I have commanded you: and, lo, I am with you always, even unto the end of the world (Matthew 28:19,20), pp. 159, 161.

APPENDIX B

FRONT-LINE ORGANIZATIONS

It is essential that those who are or wish to be engaged in the battles for America's survival do so armed with the best and most authoritative, researched information. There are many front-line organizations which qualify, but only a handful are necessary to get you started. They are leaders of vast achievement and intellect. Surround yourself with these organizations; think of them as your personal research centers or "think tanks," and your Christian Biblical Worldview will come together in every vital issue.

As you gain knowledge, they can guide you in the most effective and focused courses of action in the battle zone of your choice and calling. If you are really serious about wanting to "do something," you need look no further. You will soon find other organizations that you may wish to contact. There is an interlacing among those in the battle, and they freely recommend each other.

Let's get you started by profiling a few of them.

(1) SUMMIT MINISTRIES, P.O. Box 207, Manitou Springs, CO 80829, (719) 685-9103, Dr. David A. Noebel, Founder/President.

I can speak firsthand about the "Summit," having known Dr. Noebel for at least twenty-five years and witnessed the results of the transformation of many lives. Through the Summit, he has had an incredible impact on nearly 30,000 young graduates in every area of life - business, national defense, education, economics,

church, media, science and politics. The Summit is un-
doubtedly the most effective Christian, conservative youth
leadership training center in America. My wife and I
know. Our own children are graduates of the Summit's
concentrated 2-week summer training programs and
consider the "Summit experience" to have been a high-
light of their lives that has already paid priceless divi-
dends. When a young person graduates from the Summit, he or she (ages 16 to 25) possesses a solidly Christian
Worldview, understands the elements of the conflicts in
life's theaters, how to take the lead and win. The stories
of their triumphs in high schools, colleges and universities are boundless. Summit graduates are the liberal
socialist professors' worst nightmares.

Guest lecturers include the best of the best in our
cause of Christ and America. They are professors, theologians, military experts, scientists, leaders preeminent
in their fields. Dr. Noebel himself is known around the
world for his classic books, his latest titled *Understanding the Times,* (a comparison of Marxist, humanist and
Christian worldviews) which has become part of the
junior/senior curriculum in most of the Christian schools
of America and now is flooding the educational systems
in numerous countries of the world. Dr. D. James Kennedy
has called this book the greatest work of its kind in our
century.

What can You do? First, write to Dr. David A. Noebel,
Summit Ministries, and ask for an information packet.
They offer books (classics that are "must" reading for
action-oriented patriots), cassette tapes, whole courses
on video, all manner of seminars around the nation.
There are a hundred things that you can do right where
you are. Just let them know and ask for help. They will
help you to help America, especially our future leaders.

If you do nothing more than write for information,
you will soon find confusion and despair giving way to
hope, commitment, light, a new energy and things to do

which can make a difference...a very big difference for America.

Through the Summit you will also discover what many other organizations in our cause are doing. Their leaders lecture at the Summit. Dr. Noebel wants his graduates to be fully familiar with what the other front-line organizations are doing.

(2) WALLBUILDERS -   P.O. Box 397, Aledo, TX 76008, For orders only, call 1-800-873-2845; All other calls: 817-441-6044, David Barton, Founder/President.

Through his videos, audio cassettes, TV appearances, seminars, books and other publications, David Barton is making an inestimable contribution toward arming the American people with detailed knowledge of our sacred heritage. This prepares them to maximize their effectiveness in church, the political arenas, the schoolboards, etc.. The blessings that bond the family unit itself are transcendent of actual description because their essence is Spiritual.

Tens of thousands of home schoolers use Barton's classic video tapes. They are so extensively researched and professionally produced that everyone from children to formally educated history majors and politicians find them to be inspiring treasures. If you have children or grandchildren, I urge you to write to David Barton for his catalog of products. There are two videotapes that I would specifically recommend: "The Spirit of the American Revolution" and "America's Godly Heritage".

Two of David Barton's best books, complete with statistical charts on the social results of removing prayer and Bible reading from our schools including details on unprecedented U.S. Supreme Court cases, are *To Pray or Not To Pray*, and *Original Intent* (separation of church and state). These are must reading.

What can you do? (1) Order the catalog; (2) order the two tapes and watch them yourself; (3) order additional

copies and lend or give them to friends on the condition
that your friends promise to watch them and report back
to you. I assure you that when a friend, even a flaming
liberal, watches these video tapes, you will likely have a
convert. They are that good and persuasive.

There is no end to what you can do with Barton's
products. Never again will you be in a position of wonder-
ing, "What can I do for my faith and my country?" You,
now having direction and fine products, are the only
limitation to that answer. God has made clear what He
expects of us - total commitment to action.

Your knowledge will flow directly into every arena -
church, school, university, politics. You'll be armed and,
if you do your homework, formidable. You will truly be
the *salt* and *light* that Jesus commands you to be.

(3) *AMERICA'S GOD AND COUNTRY Encyclopedia Of Quotations,* AMERISEARCH, Inc., P.O. Box 20163, St. Louis, MO 63123, 1-888-USA-WORD, William J. Federer, Author/President.

This book has no equal among books of its kind in
America. It is a *must* for students of all ages, professors,
historians, politicians, home studies, churches, and every American citizen. No liberal professor or teacher
would stand a chance against a student armed with the
information in this book.

Its 700 pages reveal astounding reports of the profes-
sional achievements and Spiritual convictions of the
Founders of America. The real, thrilling, mostly sup-
pressed story behind famous episodes from history will
come to life.

What can you do? Order this book. Once you have
discovered the merit of my commentary above, order a
case of them, as I did, and either sell them dollar for dollar
or give them away to those who can maximize their use.
Then require reporting back to you. When you have
opened these pages, you will not be able to put the book
down. What *you* can do will soon become obvious.

(4) The PROVIDENCE FOUNDATION, P.O. Box 6759, Charlottesville, VA 22906, (804) 978-4535, Stephen McDowell, President.

This is one of our nation's greatest action-oriented American heritage foundations, and its outreach is world-wide. Part of its mission statement is "Equipping Christians to Fulfill Their Calling in Home, Church and State." The foundation offers seminars, books, Christian history tours (especially in Washington), audio cassettes and video tapes, summer institute, newsletters. Write for their list of products and ask what you can do.

(5) PETER MARSHALL MINISTRIES, 36 Nickerson Road, Orleans, MA 02653, 1-800-879-3298, Peter Marshall, Founder/President.

Yale-educated Reverend Peter Marshall is the famous son of the U.S. Senate chaplain of the same name. Co-author of several books and author of an outstanding audio/video series entitled "Restoring America," he travels throughout the country speaking to audiences large and small of the need to recover our Christian heritage and how Christians can be used of God to restore America. His product list is long and varied, but if I were to choose a favorite, it would be his and David Manuel's classic book, *The Light and the Glory*. This is a thriller about God's hand in American history from Columbus through Washington's presidency. Did you know, for example, that one of the slogans during the War for Independence was "No king but King Jesus!"? You'll read about it among the other treasures in this 359 page book, which has sold over 500,000 copies.

One of Peter Marshall's other products is a spiral-bound desk-sized flip calendar that on every page either relates an incident from our history that reveals God's hand or a quote from a famous American about his or her faith in Christ. You don't have to read a book to experience the reality of our Christian heritage. One minute a day will do it.

(6) The INSTITUTE FOR CREATION RESEARCH, ICR Ministries, Box 2667, El Cajon, CA 92021, 1-800-628-7640. Web address: http://www.ICR.ORG, Dr. Henry M. Morris, Founder/President Emeritus.

Perhaps the deadliest product of atheist, humanist John Dewey's Progressive Education has been the opening of the floodgates in America's schools to the teaching of the theory of evolution as scientific fact. It is deadly because it represents a direct attack upon the Biblical presentation of special creation by a loving, purposeful God. Evolution offers the young mind purposelessness, dog-eat-dog survival of the fittest, life by the sword with no eternal values and no future judgment, thus no accountability. Hitler, Mao Tse Tung, Ho Chi Minh, Pol Pot, Stalin, Lenin and other tyrants throughout history had to be evolutionists of one shade or another in order to justify their genocide and purges of countless millions of men, women and children. Over many decades evolutionism increasingly has entrenched itself in America's educational institutions as the Abandonment Clergy either participated or stood impotently on the sidelines as spectators.

Years ago, a Christian professor and scientist, Dr. Henry M. Morris, Chairman of the Civil Engineering Dept. at Virginia Polytechnic Institute, in witnessing firsthand the impact of the theory of evolution on the minds and worldview of his students, founded the Institute for Creation Research. He dedicated it, and his life, to countering the devastation on our culture by the evolutionists.

Dr. Morris gathered into his association a number of well-qualified scientists in all of the scientific disciplines including astrophysics, biology, archeology, chemistry, biochemistry, hydrology, engineering, physics and many other fields, such as history and theology.

Their objective was and is to produce state-of-the-art scientific evidence that the Bible is far more believable and reasonable than the "theory" of evolution. To present evolution as being the only "scientific" model for the existence of life is a deadly, destructive fraud on society.

The outreach of ICR has spread around the world, and now it has its own nationally accredited science graduate school. Its products, books, videos, audio cassettes, regular publications, its speaking and debating teams, and radio programs continue to reach and arm millions of Americans to do battle with the evolutionists. The victories have been stunning.

Of all his personal, classic books perhaps the greatest is the one just published, *The Defender's Study Bible, King James Version, Defending the Faith from a Literal Creationist Viewpoint*. Beginning in Genesis, Dr. Morris presents scientific evidence that settles the crucial questions of the "Day Age Theory" versus six solar days of creation and weaves all of the books of the Bible together to show that in context there are no so-called "contradictions" and that scientifically the Bible is more eminently logical than the impersonal random chance assumptions of evolution.

Events of creation are not repeatable and thus are not provable. But when they are presented in the context of scientific statements in the Bible that are provable and which would have been impossible for the writers to know except by Divine inspiration, "Scientific Creationism" becomes a distinctly more reasonable postulation than evolution. A modern-day Christian who reads Dr. Morris's book will find him/herself ready for battle and equipped with a winning defense of the faith against the toughest adversaries.

The Defender's Bible offers you a deep and penetrating understanding of what has been happening to our youth and how to recapture lost ground. This science-based Bible is a battle weapon of the first order in numerous realms: spiritual, ideological, political.

Be sure to order the Defender's Bible and ICR's product catalog and request to be put on their mailing list.

(7) MARLIN MADDOUX' *POINT OF VIEW* Talk Show, International Christian Media, P.O. Box 30, Dallas, TX 75221, 1-800-227-1444, Marlin Maddoux, Founder/President.

Marlin Maddoux is one of America's foremost Christian, conservative talk show hosts. He broadcasts daily on over 300 radio stations coast to coast. His interviews are with the top movers and shakers of our cause in every action arena - from political to religious.

Call his 800 number and ask for the call letters, frequency and time of his broadcasts in your area. This is a highly effective way to fine-tune your understanding of crucial events as they are happening, often in a context of history. It will help you determine your calling and how you can best serve the cause of America. Ask for his catalog of leading-edge books and video products.

(8) CORAL RIDGE PRESBYTERIAN CHURCH/ CORAL RIDGE MINISTRIES, P.O. Box 40, Ft. Lauderdale, FL 33302, 1-800-229-9673, Dr. D. James Kennedy, Sr. Minister.

If you want to see Christian action in the thick of the fight for America, write to Dr. Kennedy and ask to be put on his mailing list. No charge. It will prove to be one of the most exciting, informative, inspiring adventures of your life. Dr. Kennedy is the author and creator of Evangelism Explosion and Youth Evangelism Explosion that cross denominational lines, win millions of people to Christ, teach them how to evangelize the Word and become effective warriors for Christ. It is the first ministry to be established in every single nation on earth.

This ministry is so mammoth that pages would be required to detail it. The weekly "Coral Ridge Hour" television program is seen on more than 520 television stations, and Dr. Kennedy's daily radio programs, "Truths That Transform" and the "Kennedy Commentary" are heard on more than 500 stations, making 4,195 radio broadcasts a week. On nearly every program Dr. Kennedy interviews political, religious, scientific, educational or other leaders of our cause, giving them mass exposure throughout America and into over 58 countries.

If you write and ask to be put on his mailing list, you'll soon gain a clear understanding of the crucial issues of our times, be they the battles over abortion, homosexuality, collapsing military defenses, the ACLU's relentless attacks on our Christian heritage, U.S. Supreme Court renderings or secularism in the classroom. Dr. Kennedy doesn't just "inform and expose." He attacks!

Thank the Lord your mailbox will be constantly receiving something new from Coral Ridge. That particular freedom is a treasure and a blessing which we still can enjoy and which must be defended no matter what the cost. Once you have been on the Coral Ridge mailing list for a while, never again will you ponder the questions, "Is there hope?" or "What can I do?"

(9) THE HERITAGE FOUNDATION, 214 Massachusetts Avenue, N.E., Washington, D.C. 20002-4999, 1-800-544-4843, Dr. Edwin Feulner, President.

This is a "think tank" which draws upon the greatest minds in America for its authority. Its "mission is to formulate and promote conservative public policies based on the principles of free enterprise, limited government, traditional American values, and a strong national defense." These in fact are all Christian Worldview principles, and I have found The Heritage Foundation's studies to be of inestimable value, particularly in matters of economics and national defense. If you wish to know precisely where America stands on missile defenses and who is doing what, write for Heritage's study entitled *Defending America: A Near and Long-Term Plan To Deploy Missile Defenses*. The sixteen contributors are the elite in the defense and intelligence agencies. The

"Preface to the Study" includes this statement: "What is being challenged today [is] the Clinton Administration's policy of intentionally leaving American cities and territory open to missile attack."

I urge you to write to Heritage, The Publications Department, and ask for their list of publications. As you prepare to engage in the struggle to save America, it is essential that you establish ongoing information sources of the highest credibility. Heritage is one of them. Your routes to effective action will become evident.

(10) HIGH FRONTIER, 2800 Shirlington Road, Suite 405, Arlington, VA 22206, (703) 671-4111, FAX (703) 931-6432.

This is the organization which pioneered the concept behind the Strategic Defense Initiative, popularly known as "Star Wars," launched by President Reagan. It was founded by the late General Daniel O. Graham, USA, Ret., former Director of the Defense Intelligence Agency. High Frontier is now chaired by Ambassador Henry F. Cooper, who was Director of the Strategic Defense Initiative Organization (SDIO) in the Bush Administration.

The SDI technology employs orbiting satellites as launch bases for super fast kinetic energy non-nuclear rockets designed to intercept and destroy long-range ballistic missiles anywhere in the world, in most cases long before those ICBMs are over American territory. Those attacking missiles can be armed with as many as ten independently targeted nuclear, chemical or biological warheads destined for American cities. The intercept and destroy technology has been perfected. This is the defense that President Clinton refused to authorize while numerous Third World nations acquired, and continue to acquire, warheads and delivery systems.

There could be no better source of information for students and professionals about space warfare and how SDI could defend our cities from attacking missiles than High Frontier. They'll also direct you in the most effective courses of action and influence at every level. Write or call for their literature.

(11) THE McALVANY INTELLIGENCE ADVISOR, P.O. Box 84904, Phoenix, AZ 85071, 1-800-525-9556, Don McAlvany, Founder/Editor.

Mr. Don McAlvany is the Editor of "The McAlvany Intelligence Advisor," a geopolitical/investment newsletter read by thousands of key governmental and military leaders, opinion makers, private individuals and other influential people in Washington and some 50 countrics across the free world. Throughout the pages of his newsletter, he provides in-depth analyses of world events and their investment implications.

If you wonder what the connection is between political movements and world economics, this is probably the best, most authoritative intelligence report in the nation. In fact Don McAlvany does exhaustive research into all of the principal players on the world stage and spells them out in his "Advisor." Today's momentous events are constantly cast in the framework of history back to the earliest recordings, and almost every issue contains a treasure house of quotations from the greatest men of the past to those making history today. Tomorrow is anticipated by the past together with current events, often within the framework of Biblical prophecy. This is a *must* publication for serious students and anybody intent on helping save our country.

(12) THE CONSERVATIVE CAUCUS FOUNDATION, INC., 450 Maple Avenue East, Vienna, VA 22180, (703) 281-6782, Howard Phillips, Founder/President.

Truly one of America's great research foundations, Conservative Caucus specializes in researching and producing analyses of the hottest political and freedom issues of the day. Opinions are based upon what is

Constitutionally correct, recognizing that civil and moral laws are rooted in the truth of the Scriptures. Available research papers include subjects such as government funding of homosexuals, NAFTA, abortion, START I and START II defense treaties, Panama Canal after 1999. In fact this is a priceless information source about bills before the Congress on any important subject from education to defense.

THE CONSERVATIVE CAUCUS, INC., 450 Maple Avenue East, Vienna, VA 22180, (703) 938-9626, Howard Phillips, Chairman.

Separate from the Foundation above, The Conservative Caucus is a grassroots lobbying organization to inform Americans about the struggle to restore our federal government to its Biblical premises and Constitutional boundaries. TCC has worked to cut federal spending, slash taxes, eliminate regulations, strengthen America's defenses, end ideological patronage and preserve our national independence.

(13) THERE'S NO PLACE LIKE HOME, INC. P.O. Box 631, Fredericktown, MO 63645, (314) 521-8487

Educators, authors, speakers and leaders, Jon and Candy Summers have inspired, educated, encouraged and faithfully served the homeschooling community since 1987. Leading with a vision to train godly generations, Jon and Candy continue to help thousands of families fulfill God's greatest calling to raise godly children through workshops, conferences, conventions and their magazine *There's No Place Like Home.*

Drawing upon America's finest authors, speakers, lawyers, pastors, educators and mothers, this outstanding magazine covers a wealth of inspirational and informative articles on child training, marriage, walking with God and leadership. America's biblical heritage, legislative issues and alerts, educational materials, the blessings of homeschooling, unit studies, how to teach, creation science, travel, surprising and delighting, decorating, cooking and parties.

To receive a trial issue, please send a check or money order for $4.00 to *There's No Place Like Home,* P.O. Box 613, Fredericktown, MO 63645.

(14) KOINONIA HOUSE, P.O. Box-D, Coeur d' Alene, ID 83816, 1-800-KHOUSE-1, Chuck Missler, Founder.

Chuck Missler, founder of Koinonia House, is a renowned Bible teacher and is considered to be one of America's foremost "spiritual watchmen," alerting the Body of Christ of deceptions that could affect their spirituality and lifestyle. His military and CEO background gives him an added insight into prophecy and world events from a Biblical perspective.

Chuck's ministry is dedicated to "Preparing the Body of Christ for the NEW MILLENNIUM" by providing Bible studies with great insight and numerous resources to assist both laypeople and ministers with information that will help them to stay current on what is happening worldwide. His resources include "Personal UPDATE," a monthly news journal (first year free) that is one of the most comprehensive reports on various subjects of interest to concerned Christians. Covered are articles on science and technology, world news, prophecy and relationships. Others are "The Missler Report," a weekly recording of his radio program on crucial issues and events, "K-RATIONS," a weekly world perspective update and Bible study on cassette tape, his radio broadcasts, "66/40" and "The Missler Report," and Internet websites, www.khouse.org, and www.AudioCentral.com that provide on-line teaching and ministry programs that can be heard any time at the listener's discretion.

Abandonment Theology: The Clergy and the Decline of American Christianity

Briefing Package

Now you can listen to this crucial message from John Chalfant explaining our current American spiritual and political meltdown on cassette tape! Edited to cover the highlights on two audiocassettes, you can listen to this message in your car or share it with friends. This is "must hearing" if you cherish your freedom and religious heritage.

Two cassette tapes in an album, $14.95.
To order, call 1-800-KHOUSE-1.

Listen to the AudioBook version of
Abandonment Theology on AudioCentral.com!

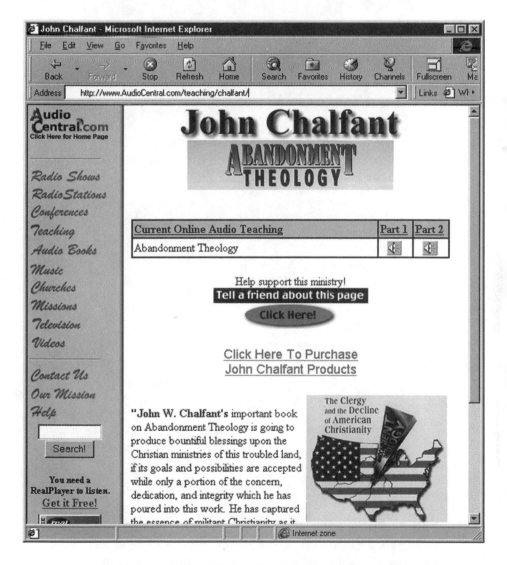

Go to - http://www.AudioCentral.com
Internet Broadcasting from a Christian Perspective:
Daily News, Bible Studies, Music and MovieGuide Movie Reviews.

"Personal UPDATE" News Journal
By Chuck Missler

The News Journal of Koinonia House   Volume 8, No. 12, December 1998

A Letter from the Editors:

Dear Friend in Christ:

Once again we find ourselves in the season of nostalgic memories, warm friendships, and family gatherings. It is a time for holiday celebrations and a break from our usual routines. And it is a time for reexamining the year that has passed and reflecting on the horizon just ahead.

It may be a challenge to fend off the holiday pressures and not let the hassles of the season keep us from enjoying the opportunities these days present. (To assist in you in your search for "relevant gifts," we have included a few suggestions in the center section.)

Some attribute our tradition of the giving of gifts at this time of year to the gifts of the Magi to the Babe in Bethlehem. However, if we really want to emulate that occasion, we should be giving gifts to *Him*, not to each other! Why not make this holiday season the occasion of offering something special *to the King we celebrate:* perhaps an indulgence we know we ought to doff; a habit that needs a firmer resolve; or, even better, *our very selves,* in some form of renewed commitment...

What better way to clear our paths in preparation for the special challenges that the coming New Year will bring?

In His Name,

Chuck and Nancy Missler

Receive a one-year subscription to Chuck Missler's monthly "Personal UPDATE," an informative monthly news journal by Bible teacher, watchman of world events in prophecy, and Y2K expert - Chuck Missler. This is a $20 value, free to you as a first-time subscriber. Call 1-800-KHOUSE-1 to order.

APPENDIX C

ABOUT THE AUTHOR

Many years of reading, research and inner-circle associations with America's great spiritual, military and conservative leaders have brought John W. Chalfant numerous awards and recognitions but more importantly have resulted in his insight into the spiritual crises afflicting virtually every aspect of our personal and national lives.

For most of his youth his first love was electronics, secondarily political affairs. His foremost political "hero" was Richard Arens, Staff Director of the House Committee on Un-American Activities, who had produced a research series on Soviet world expansion. Next was J. Edgar Hoover, Director of the F.B.I.

While working at a missile research and development center, a senior colleague played a tape-recording for Chalfant of a speech by Arens titled, "Dangers to our Internal Security." Arens began, "Two thousand years ago there was One who spoke these words: 'No man can serve two masters' ..." The first fifteen minutes were devoted to comparing Jesus Christ, the Author of freedom, to Karl Marx, the destroyer of freedom. That speech transformed Chalfant's life, and he committed the rest of it to the service of Jesus Christ and America's freedoms.

Chalfant began his new career by organizing and directing the award-winning statewide (Delaware) "Freedom on the Offense" program, recognized by J. Edgar Hoover and others. Over the next thirty years he developed personal associations with many of the Christian,

conservative and pro-defense leaders of national movements whom he helped in many ways, especially funding.
He settled in Miami, opened a commercial real estate
company specializing in syndications and land development and with his wife raised five wonderful children.
Chalfant was asked by the American Security Council to
head its national pro-defense "SALT Syndrome" video
marketing campaign, which President-elect Ronald
Reagan later wrote was a major factor in his election
victory. He was also invited to join the Council for
National Policy.

This background culminated in his authoring *Abandonment Theology*, the first in a series of hard-hitting
analysis and solutions-oriented books, studies and position papers to be published under the nationally trade-
marked name, America - A Call to Greatness® of which
John Chalfant is Founder/President. It is one product in
a complex of worldwide marketing and support outlets
including the Internet.

APPENDIX D

ACKNOWLEDGMENTS

The Story Behind the Book

If this book were a beginning and ending in itself, expressing thanks and appreciation to some key people directly involved in its production and editing would be a simple and brief matter. But such is not the case. *Abandonment Theology*, published by America - A Call to Greatness, Inc., is only one product in a complex of support efforts. The book was conceived several years ago and is the first in a series of books, studies and position papers on America's Christian heritage, what has brought her to the brink of the abyss and how to restore her to a new height of greatness.

So many people are involved in the total effort that naming each of them and showing proper appreciation is impossible. At the risk of offense to some, I'll name a few who have been most directly involved in the book effort.

The book got off to a strange start. Three years ago Bill Ball, a leader in the prestigious Council For National Policy, asked me to write a brochure about a vision I had for a full-length book to be called America - A Call to Greatness for a special presentation he would make to 200 national leaders. Howard Phillips (founder, Conservative Caucus), Dr. Henry M. Morris (founder, Institute for Creation Research), Dr. David Noebel (founder, Summit Ministries), and Dr. D. J. Kennedy (founder/Sr.

Minister, Coral Ridge Presbyterian Church) went on the line in my eight-panel brochure with supporting statements.

As I began writing the book, my supporters and I realized that marketing was crucial because it does little good to write an important work if it never gets out of its own back yard. We decided to produce a one-hour video special titled *America - A Call To Greatness* about America's Christian heritage, to be televised nationwide in the Christian markets. This would pave the way for the book through name recognition. We formed a production company and contracted with an independent video producer who brought in a number of America's most popular Christian singing talent and many of the greatest leaders of our cause to protect America's God-given freedoms. We began filming at Disney/MGM Studios.

It soon became obvious that the markets were far beyond what we had anticipated or were capable of handling, so a new production company, Paige-Brace Cinema Ltd./Joe and Susan Hilyard, took over and, together with new producer/director/writer Dr. Warren H. Chaney, produced an outstanding network-quality two hour video which included all of the original participants, hosted by Charlton Heston and featuring famous personalities such as Peter Graves, Mickey Rooney, Gene Autry and many more, three former U.S. Presidents and politicians such as Steve Stockman and Alan Keyes. It will be shown first throughout America, then in many countries.

A special 2-hour spinoff edition tailored slightly for the Christian markets is titled *Mine Eyes Have Seen The Glory - America Calls*. This is being advertised by Marlin Maddoux and others. These video productions are independent of the books, yet they serve the envisioned trailblazing purpose.

Now with all of that under way, back to the books and the one at hand, *Abandonment Theology*. My vision for the described, hard-hitting book on America's heritage, problems and cures, culminated over thirty years of help given to many of the premier leaders of our cause of Christ and America's freedoms.

Others caught the vision: Glen and Georgia Lindengren, Col. Wes and Jean Pennington, Bob and Donna Schumaker, Dr. and Mrs. Enslie Schilb, Bob Wilson, Ron and Margaret Black contributed the startup funds in addition to our own.

There were several protracted hard times, black clouds and storms. More than once during those dark hours when everything seemed lost, a Providentially-timed letter would arrive from Dr. D. James Kennedy reminding me to place my absolute trust in God, with full faith that He would see us through. I did. He did.

Clearly, God's hand was on this work because every crisis brought in its wake huge expansions, encouragement and unexpected funding. Bob Truitt, George and Sandra Joseph, Bill and Jackie Leppert, Dr. Jerome Harold, Lowell and Nancy Dotson, Bob and Shirley Staib, Eugene Horvath, Col. Stanley Hand, Lucille Hardy, C.B. Van Alstine, Col. Eugene and Dorothea Minietta, Walter "Bucky" Allen, Gen. Robert Richardson, Ron Cole, Larry Zagray, David and Marta McDuffie, Gen. John and Joan Singlaub, Col. Ron Ray, Judith Reisman, Ph.D., Elaine Donnelly - all extended their help in many ways. The list of wonderful, faithful men and women goes on.

I am also grateful to Washington attorney Jim Guirard, widely published in *The Wall Street Journal* and other major periodals on defense issues; Sven Kraemer, one of America's leading defense analysts (his credentials are in the subsection "Soviet Smoke..." Chapter Three); Dr. Joe Douglass, highly respected military analyst, authority in chemical and biological warfare, who was most helpful in editing said military presentation. These men have long been friends and consultants.

Thanks also to Bill Federer for permitting us to draw biographies and quotations from his classic book, *AMERICA'S GOD AND COUNTRY Encyclopedia of Quotations;* to David Barton, founder of WallBuilders, Inc., for supplying Figures 2 through 6 in Chapter Two, showing the impact on the lives of young people when in 1962 the U.S. Supreme Court effectively outlawed prayer and Bible reading in the public schools, and to Dr. Edwin Feulner, President, The Heritage Foundation, for supplying the defense charts.

Special thanks also to Dr. David Noebel for his review of the original manuscript and his excellent suggestions. If ever special honor should be given to anyone, it goes to my mother who has never once flinched in her steadfast support.

I must admit, however, that the faith of every one combined could not match that of my priceless dauntless wife Linda and our five children - Leetha, Katherine, Elizabeth, John, Jr., and Christine, who committed all of their personal resources to help "seed" the initial video project. This book and their commitment have been an endless source of inspiration to me. They know the perils ahead for our freedoms and have been willing to sacrifice many luxuries in order to do everything possible in the commission of their sacred duty to our country and for their future children.

In overview when we consider the professions of those named above, they sound much like those of the Founding Fathers. Among them are physicians, attorneys, university professors, Ph.D.s, scientists, military generals, historians, clergymen, presidents of academic institutions, industrialists, businessmen and land developers. In contemporary terms, two former Strategic Air Command (SAC) Wing Commanders, even an IRS executive (ready to retire), politicians (all good guys). To all of these great men and women, and those to come, we offer our eternal thanks. This is only the beginning.

Endnotes

1. Ronald H. Nash, *Worldviews in Conflict* (Grand Rapids, MI:Zondervan Publishing House, 1992), back cover.

2. D. James Kennedy, *Defending the First Amendment* (Ft. Lauderdale, FL:Coral Ridge Ministries, 1989), p. 16.

3. Lucile Johnston, *Celebrations of a Nation* (Huntsville, AL:Johnston Bicentennial Foundation, 1987), p. 130.

4. W. Cleon Skousen, *The Making of America: The Substance and Meaning of the Constitution* (Washington:The National Center for Constitutional Studies, 1985), p. 1.

5. Karl Marx and Friedrich Engles, *The Communist Manifesto* (New York:Review Press, Modern Reader Paperbacks, 1964), p. 39.

6. Fisher Ames, *The Works of Fisher Ames,* W. B. Allen, Ed., Vol. I, "Essays on Social Class and Character" (Indianapolis: Liberty Classics, 1983), p. 37.

7. James Madison, "The Federalist #10" in Alexander Hamilton, John Jay, James Madison, *The Federalist on the New Constitution* (Philadelphia:Benjamin Warner, 1818), p. 53.

8. Charles Francis Adams, *The Works of John Adams* (Boston:Little and Brown, 1851), p. 10.

9. "The Declaration of Independence, 1776" in *The People Shall Judge, Readings in the Formation of American Policy, Vol. 1,* Selected and Edited by The Staff, Social Sciences 1, The College of the University of Chicago (Chicago:The University of Chicago Press, 1949), p. 200.

10. William J. Federer, *America's God and Country Encyclopedia of Quotations* (Coppell, TX:Fame Publishing, 1994), p. 9.

11. William J.Federer, p. 23.

12. George Morgan, *Patrick Henry* (Philadelphia:J. B. Lippincott Co., 1929), p. 189-191.

13. *American Quotations* (Avenel, NJ:Wings Books, 1992), p. 157.

14. William J. Federer, p. 411.

15. John Witherspoon, *The Works of John Witherspoon, VOL. IV* (London:Ogles, Duncan and Cochran, 1815), p. 209-216.

16. Reverend August J. Kling, from a sermon entitled "Liberty and Law," First Presbyterian Church, Miami, FL, July 9, 1972.

17. William J. Federer, p. 205.

18. William J. Federer, p. 481.

19. Mark A. Beliles and Stephen K. McDowell, *America's Providential History* (Charlottesville, VA:Providence Foundation, 1989), p. 90.

20. Henry M. Morris, *Many Infallible Proofs,* (El Cajon, CA:Creation-Life Publisher, Inc., 1974), p. 20.

21. *Church of the Holy Trinity v. U.S.;* 143 U.S., 457, 465-471 (1892).

22. William J. Federer, p. 331.

23. William J. Federer, p. 657.

24. William J. Federer, p. 658.

25. William J. Federer, p. 658.

26. William J. Federer, p. 410.

27. William J. Federer, p. 216.

28. Robert Flood, *America God Shed His Grace on Thee* (Chicago:Moody Bible Institute, Moody Press, 1975), p. 160.

29. D. James Kennedy, p. 16.

30. Kling sermon.

31. John Witherspoon, *The Works of John Witherspoon, VOL. IX* (London:Ogles, Duncan and Cochran, 1815), H3.

32. David A. Noebel, *Understanding the Times* (Manitou Springs, CO:Summit Press, 1991), p. 522.

33. David Noebel, p. 200.

34. David Noebel, p. 203.

35. D. James Kennedy, letter to constituents, July 26, 1983.

36. D. James Kennedy letter, 1983.

37. D. James Kennedy, *Defending the First Amendment*, p. 20-21.

38. D. James Kennedy, *Defending the First Amendment*, p. 21.

39. D. James Kennedy, *Defending the First Amendment*, p. 22.

40. D. James Kennedy, *Defending the First Amendment*, p. 22.

41. D. James Kennedy, *Defending the First Amendment,* Kennedy, p. 27. Also David Barton, *The Myth of Separation.* Aledo, TX:WallBuilders Press, 1991, p. 12.

42. William J. Federer, p. 411.

43. David Barton, *America: To Pray? Or Not to Pray?* (Aledo, TX:WallBuilder Press, 1994), p. 46.

44. David Barton, *America: To Pray? Or Not to Pray?* p. 47.

45. David Barton, *The Myth of Separation,* (Aledo, TX:WallBuilder Press, 1991), p. 49.

46. David Barton, *America: To Pray? Or Not to Pray?* p. 51.

47. David Barton, *America: To Pray? Or Not to Pray?* p. 52.

48. "The Salt Syndrome" a videotape and transcript of the Salt II hearings before the Senate Foreign Relations Committee, July 31, 1979 hearings, video produced by The American Security Council Education Foundation, Boston, VA., 1980, p. 17.

49. George Canning, *Bartlett's Familiar Quotations,* John
    Bartlett, Ed. (Boston:Little, Brown and Company, Inc., 1968),
    p. 506.

50. John A. Stormer, *None Dare Call it Treason/25 Years Later*
    (Florissant, MO:Liberty Bell Press, 1990), p. 75.

51. R. J. Rummel, *Lethal Politics* (New Brunswick,
    NJ:Transaction Publishers, 1990), p. xi.

52. R. J. Rummel, p. 5.

53. U.S. Department of State, "Freedom from War: The United
    States Program for General and Complete Disarmament in a
    Peaceful World," Department of State Publication 7277,
    (Washington:Sup't. of Documents, U.S. Gov't. Printing Office,
    1961,) 0-609147.

54. Rep. Weiss, *Congressional Record,* May 25, 1982, H2840-
    H2849.

55. U.S. Department of Defense, *Soviet Military Power: 1990*
    (Washington:U.S. Printing Office, 1990), p. 88.

56. "The Salt Syndrome," American Security Council video tape
    transcript, p. 2.

57. John A. Stormer, p. 221.

58. Robert Morris, *Our Globe Under Siege, III* (Mantoloking, NJ:J
    & W Enterprises, 1988), p. 182.

59. "The Salt Syndrome," American Security Council video tape
    transcript, p. 17.

60. Quentin Crommelin, Jr. and David S. Sullivan, *Soviet Mili-
    tary Supremacy* (Los Angeles:University of Southern Califor-
    nia, 1985), p. 25.

61. The Heritage Foundation, *Defending America: A Near- and
    Long-Term Plan to Deploy Missile Defenses* (Washington:The
    Heritage Foundation, 1995), p. 1.

62. The Heritage Foundation, p. 1.

63. "Aspin writes 'Star Wars' obituary," *The Orlando Sentinel,* 14 May, 1993: A3.

64. Rep. Floyd D. Spence, Report on Full Committee Hearing on Ballistic Missile Defense, March 14, 1996, p. 2.

65. W. Cleon Skousen, *The Naked Communist* (Salt Lake City:The Reviewer, 1978), p. 208.

66. Donald S. McAlvany, *The McAlvany Intelligence Advisor,* Phoenix, AZ, Fall, 1989, 1.

67. Joseph D. Douglass, Ph.D., Falls Church, VA, correspondence with the author, 1996. Dr. Douglass is an authority on military affairs and weapons systems.

68. Donald S. McAlvany, *The McAlvany Intelligence Advisor,* Phoenix, AZ, April, 1996, p. 22.

69. Bill Gertz, "Russian nuclear exercises include mock hit on U.S.," *Washington Times,* 14 September, 1993, np.

70. Joseph D. Douglass, 1996.

71. The Heritage Foundation, *The Defense Budget Debate: Is Bush Asking the Right Questions?* (Washington:The Heritage Foundation, 1991), p. 5.

72. The Heritage Foundation, p. 16.

73. C-SPAN televised hearing, Senate Armed Services Committee Hearing on Defense Budget, 21 February, 1991.

74. Bruce B. Auster and Stephen Budiansky, "Tomorrow," *U.S. News and World Report,* 23 September, 1991, p. 39.

75. Kevin Fedarko, "Time for Battling Boris," *Time,* 26 February, 1996, p. 49.

76. Floyd Spence, "Missile Defense Vacuity," *Washington Times,* 29 February, 1996, np.

77. Joseph D. Douglass, 1996.

78. *The People Shall Judge,* (Chicago:University of Chicago Press, 1949), p. 210.

79. *The People Shall Judge,* p. 8.

80. John A. Eidsmoe, "The Legal Feasibility of the Ban," in *Caveat,* ed. David W. Dunham (Franklin, TN:Legacy Communications, 1993), p. 68.

81. John A. Eidsmoe, p. 68.

82. Chandler Burr, "Friendly Fire," *California Lawyer,* June, 1994: 54.

83. Adm. Thomas Moorer (Ret.), Former Chairman of the Joint Chiefs of Staff, as quoted in *The New American,* 14 Dec. 1992, p.12.

84. Marlin Maddoux, "The Seven Myths of Gay Pride," in *Caveat,* ed. David W. Dunham (Franklin, TN:Legacy Communications, 1993), p. 39.

85. Col. Ronald D. Ray, *Military Necessity & Homosexuality,* (Louisville:First Principles, Inc., 1993), p. 65.

86. Col. Ronald D. Ray, p. 42.

87. "Gay Re-Education for U.S. Servicemen?" *Lambda Report,* June-July, 1993:p. 1.

88. Col. Ronald D. Ray, "Lifting the Ban on Homosexuals in the Military: The Subversion of a Moral Principle," in *Gays and Lesbians in the Military,* ed. Wilbur J. Scott and Sandra Carson Stanley (New York: Aldine De Gruyter, 1993), p. 97.

89. Harold M. Voth, "Foreword," in Col. Ronald D. Ray, *Military Necessity & Homosexuality* (Louisville:First Principles, Inc., 1993), p. v.

90. Correspondence with author from Judith Reisman, Ph.D., author and expert on human behavior, Oct. 3, 1996.

91. William J. Federer, p. 500.

92. Maj. Gen. John K. Singlaub, U.S. Army (Ret.) in a phone conversation with the author, October, 1996.

93. "Land Combat: The Experiment Begins," *CMR Reports,* Nov. 1994:p. 1

94. Meeting Notes, The Presidential Commission on the Assignment of Women in the Armed Forces (PCAWAF), June 25, 1992, p. 6-9.

95. Meeting Notes, PCAWAF, p. 6-9.

96. Meeting Notes, PCAWAF, p. 7.

97. Col. Ronald D. Ray, *Military Necessity & Homosexuality,* p. 18.

98. *Report to the President,* The Presidential Commission on the Assignment of Women in the Armed Forces (PCAWAF), Nov. 15, 1992, p. 46.

99. *Report to the President,* p. 47.

100. *Report to the President,* p. 47.

101. "Navy Policy on Pregnancy," *CMR Report,* March, 1995:p. 1-2.

102. "Combat for Women Deserves Closer Look," *CMR Report,* Aug. 1993:p. 1.

103. Maj. Gen. John K. Singlaub, Oct. 1996.

104. "Double Standards," *CMR Notes,* June 1995:p. 2.

105. "Land Combat: The Experiment Begins," p. 3.

106. David Noebel, p. 193.

107. Tim LaHaye, *The Battle For The Mind* (Old Tappan, NJ:Fleming H. Revell Co., 1980), Introduction.

108. Ronald H. Nash, p. 20.

109. Dr. H. Edward Rowe, Dallas, TX, correspondence with the author, 1979.

110. R. C. Sproul, *Classical Apologetics* (Grand Rapids, MI: Zondervan Publishing House, 1984), p. 5.

111. R. C. Sproul, p. 4.

112. R. C. Sproul, p. 4.

113. Adolph Hitler, *Mein Kampf* (New York:Reynal & Hitchcock, 1941), p. 327.

114. Adolph Hitler, p. 364.

115. D. James Kennedy, *Defending the First Amendment,* p. 21.

116. David Barton, *Original Intent* (Aledo, TX:WallBuilders Press, 1996), p. 14.

117. Stephen K. McDowell and Mark A. Beliles, *America's Providential History* (Charlottsville, VA:Providence Press, 1988), p. 79.

118. Madison Peters, *Haym Solomon, The Financier of the Revolution* (New York:The Throw Press, 1911), np.

119. R. C. Sproul, p. 4.

120. *Church of the Holy Trinity v. U.S.,* 465-471.

121. Richard Arens in a speech to the Daughters of the American Revolution, 1964.

122. William J. Federer, p. 18.

123. William J. Federer, p. 205.

124. Henry M. Morris, p. 12-17.

125. D. James Kennedy, *What if Jesus Had Never Been Born?* (Nashville:Thomas Nelson Publishers, 1994), p. 237-238.

Index